当代中国微记录

GLIMPSES OF CONTEMPORARY CHINA

「行在中国」

GETTING AROUND IN CHINA

李禄兴　主编
李禄兴　齐　影　编著

Chief compiler: Li Luxing
Compilers: Li Luxing　Qi Ying

SinolinguA
华语教学出版社

First Edition 2019

ISBN 978-7-5138-1639-7
Copyright 2019 by Sinolingua Co., Ltd
Published by Sinolingua Co., Ltd
24 Baiwanzhuang Road, Beijing 100037, China
Tel: (86)10-68320585 68997826
Fax: (86)10-68997826 68326333
http://www.sinolingua.com.cn
E-mail: hyjx@sinolingua.com.cn
Facebook: www.facebook.com/sinolingua
Printed by Beijing Xicheng Printing Co. Ltd

Printed in the People's Republic of China

编者的话

近年来，中国在国际上的影响力逐渐增强，很多人渴望了解中国，不仅想了解中国的古老文明，更希望了解当下的中国社会和普通中国人的日常生活。另外，随着孔子学院和孔子课堂在世界各地生根，大量学生，特别是中小学生在学习汉语过程中希望通过语言学习更直接地认识这个古老国家的今天是什么样子的。同时，笔者根据在海外多年的教学经历也体会到，如果一个学生对使用该语言的国家一无所知或知之不多，往往会影响他们对这种语言的学习兴趣。

了解中国，从细微处开始，于是有了这套“当代中国微记录”。这套书共 10 册，每一册着重介绍中国的某一方面，例如：饮食、交通、家庭，等等，针对新 HSK 水平考试 5 级以上汉语学习者，尽可能将词汇量限定在 2500-3000 范围以内，超范围词汇在词后直接加英文注释，以方便学习者阅读和理解。本套书以平民的视角、平实的语言和家长里短的故事性叙述，将当今中国的各个侧面展现在汉语学习者面前，汉语学习者可以边学汉语边达到了解现实中国的目的。为减轻学习者的畏难心理负担，每册书只有大概一万多汉字，并全部配有汉语拼音，附赠的拼音隐形卡可以给不需要拼音辅助的学习者提供帮助。书中有大量图片，便于学习者理解内容，对中国有更直观的认知。这套书可以作为孔子学院或孔子课堂的汉语教材使用，也可以做中国国情课的教材或汉语课外读物。

感知中国，从“当代中国微记录”开始！

编　者

目录 | CONTENTS

001　春运：漫漫回家路

009　公共交通：方便又实惠

016　飞机：飞入寻常百姓家

024　高速公路改变生活

030　中国进入高铁时代

037　公交一卡通：不仅仅是公交卡

043　让人堵心的堵车

050　长途车开到家门口

057　自驾游：随心而动

065　自行车的命运

Chūnyùn : Mànmàn Huíjiā Lù

春运：漫漫回家路

Chūnyùn, zhǐ Chūn Jié qījiān de lǚkè yùnshū
春运，指春节期间的旅客运输 (transportation)。

Chūnjié shì Zhōngguó zuì zhòngyào de chuántǒng jiérì. Chūnjié
春节是中国最重要的传统节日。春节

qián, rénmen dōu yào huíjiā gēn zìjǐ de fùmǔ, qīzi hé
前，人们都要回家跟自己的父母、妻子和

háizi yìqǐ guònián. Suǒyǐ Chūnjié qījiān de huǒchēpiào,
孩子一起过年。所以春节期间的火车票、

chángtú qìchēpiào, fēijīpiào děng dōu tèbié jǐnzhāng, xūyào
长途汽车票、飞机票等都特别紧张，需要

tíqián hěn duō tiān yùdìng

提前很多天预订 (make an advance booking)。

Gēnjù tǒngjì, měi nián Chūnjié qījiān, lǚkè de yùnsòng

根据统计，每年春节期间，旅客的运送

shùliàng dōu dádào liǎng-sān yì réncì. Yǒu wàiguó jìzhě shuō:

数量都达到两三亿人次。有外国记者说：

"Zhè shì rénlèi lìshǐ shang zuì dà guīmó de rénkǒu duǎnqī liúdòng."

“这是人类历史上最大规模的人口短期流动 (flow)。”

Chūnyùn yìbān cóng Chūn Jié qián tiān kāishǐ, dào Chūn Jié

春运一般从春节前10天开始，到春节

hòu tiān jiéshù. Zài bú dào yí gè yuè de shíjiān li, yào yùnsòng

后15天结束。在不到一个月的时间里，要运送

zhème duō rén, shì qítā guójiā dōu bù kěnéng yùdào de

这么多人，是其他国家都不可能遇到的

qíngkuàng. Zhè duì tiělù, mínháng, gōnglù

情况。这对铁路、民航 (civil aviation)、公路

děng bùmén dōu shì hěn dà de tiāozhàn . Rúhé zǔzhī hǎo zhè duàn
等部门都是很大的挑战。如何组织好这段

shíjiān de yùnshū , bǎozhèng lǚkè ānquán , jíshí , zhǔnshí de
时间的运输，保证旅客安全、及时、准时地

dàodá mùdìdì , shì xūyào zhìhuì hé fāngfǎ de .
到达目的地，是需要智慧 (wisdom) 和方法的。

Huǒchē shì dà duōshù rén shǒuxuǎn de jiāotōng gōngjù . Yóuyú
火车是大多数人首选的交通工具。由于

huíjiā de rén tài duō , huǒchēpiào chángcháng hěn nán mǎi , yǒude
回家的人太多，火车票常常很难买，有的

rén wèile mǎi piào yào pái yī-liǎng gè xiǎoshí de duì . Wèicǐ , tiělù
人为了买票要排一两个小时的队。为此，铁路

bùmén cǎiqǔle hěn duō cuòshī , huǎnjiě zhèzhǒng
部门采取了很多措施，缓解 (to alleviate) 这种

qíngkuàng . Lìrú dàxuéshēng shì chūnyùn de yì zhī zhǔlìjūn ,
情况。例如大学生是春运的一支主力军，

huǒchēzhàn gōngzuò rényuán jiù tíqián duō tiān , dào gègè
火车站工作人员就提前 20 多天，到各个

dàxué màipiào , píng xuéshēngzhèng kěyǐ tíqián yùdìng zìjǐ huíjiā
大学卖票，凭学生证可以提前预订自己回家

de huǒchēpiào . Zhèyàng suǒyǒu de dàxuéshēng chēpiào wèntí jiù
的火车票。这样所有的大学生车票问题就

kěyǐ jiějué le , tāmen jiù búyòng zhuānmén dào huǒchēzhàn qù
可以解决了，他们就不用专门到火车站去

páiduì mǎipiào le , zhège huódòng jiào “sòngpiào shàngmén
排队买票了，这个活动叫“送票上门 (ticket

” . Lìngwài , huǒchēpiào hái shíxíng shímíngzhì
delivery)”。另外，火车票还实行实名制 (real-

, kěyǐ zài wǎngshang mǎi .
name ticket purchasing system)，可以在 网上 买。

Zài wǎngshang tiánxiě zhēnshí xìngmíng , shēnfènzhèng hàomǎ děng
在 网上 填写 真实 姓名、 身份证 号码 等

xìnxī , yì rén yí piào , jiù kěyǐ shùnlì mǎi dào huǒchēpiào .
信息，一人一票，就可以顺利买到 火车票。

Wáng Dàchéng shì zài Shēnzhèn gōngzuò de Shāndōngrén , tā
王 大成是在 深圳 工作的 山东人，他

jiù tǐhuì dàole zhèzhǒng shòupiào fāngshì de hǎochù . Tā shuō :
就体会到了 这种 售票 方式的好处。他 说：

" Yǐqián zǎochen sìdiǎn duō qǐchuáng dào huǒchēzhàn mǎi piào ,
“以前 早晨 四点 多 起床 到 火车站 买票，

hái chángcháng mǎi bu dào . Xiànzài zhǐyào zuò zài diànnǎo qián , jiù
还 常常 买不到。现在只要坐在电脑 前，就

kěyǐ mǎi dào huǒchēpiào le , zhēnde hěn fāngbiàn . ” Huǒchēzhàn
可以买到火车票了，真的很方便。” 火车站

hái zài hěn duō dìfang shèlìle dàishòudiǎn , zài
还在很多地方设立了代售点 (sales agency)，在

zhèxiē dìfang dōu kěyǐ tíqián mǎi huǒchēpiào , ér búbì qīnzì
这些地方都可以提前买火车票，而不必亲自

dào huǒchēzhàn mǎi . Chūnjié qījiān , yóuyú
(in personal) 到火车站买。春节期间，由于

lǚkè xíngli bǐjiào duō , zài jiā shàng zuòwèi yǒuxiàn , yǒuxiē rén
旅客行李比较多，再加上座位有限，有些人

zhǐ néng mǎi dào zhànpiào . Zhèyàng
只能买到站票 (ticket for standing room)。这样

chēxiāng li jiù xiǎnde hěn yōngjǐ , dàn dàjiā dōu wèile huíjiā
车厢里就显得很拥挤，但大家都为了回家

guònián , zhǐyào zuò shàng huǒchē , xiǎngdào huíjiā gēn fùmǔ ,
过年，只要坐上火车，想到回家跟父母、

xiōngdì , zǐnǚ zài yìqǐ guònián de qíngjǐng , dàjiā yě bù juéde
兄弟、子女在一起过年的情景，大家也不觉得

yǒu shénme xīnkǔ le .
有什么辛苦了。

Chángtú kèchē yě shì yì zhǒng zhòngyào de chūnyùn
长途客车也是一种重要的春运

jiāotōng gōngjù . Chūnyùn qījiān , yóuyú lǚkè fēicháng duō ,
交通工具。春运期间，由于旅客非常多，

yǒuxiē chángtú kèchē wèile duō zhuànqián , huì chūxiàn duō lā
有些长途客车为了多赚钱，会出现多拉

lǚkè de xiànxiàng , lìrú kèchē de zuòwèi shù shì rén , ér
旅客的现象，例如客车的座位数是42人，而

shíjì shàngchē de rénshù kěnéng shì rén huòzhě gèng duō.
实际上车的人数可能是45人或者更多。
jiāotōng bùmén wèile zhìzhǐ zhèzhǒng xiànxiàng,
交通部门为了制止(to prevent)这种现象，
bǎozhèng lǚkè de ānquán, duì zhèzhǒng xiànxiàng jìnxíng yángé
保证旅客的安全，对这种现象进行严格
kòngzhì. Zài chēzhàn, lù shang dōu yǒu jiāotōng jǐngchá, huì
控制。在车站、路上都有交通警察，会
suíshí ràngchēliàng tíngxiàlai jìnxíng jiǎnchá, rúguǒ fāxiàn chāoyuán
随时让车辆停下来进行检查，如果发现超员
, yào duì kèchē
(carry more passengers than stipulated)，要对客车
sījī jìnxíng chǔfá , tongshí xièxia chāochū de rén,
司机进行处罚(to punish)，同时卸下超出的人，
yóujiāotōng jǐngchá ānpái qítā chēliàng yùnsòng.
由交通警察安排其他车辆运送。

Zuòfēijī lǚxíng xiāngduì lái shuō shì bǐjiào shūfu de. Dàn
坐飞机旅行相对来说是比较舒服的。但

Chūnjié qījiān fēijīpiào de jiàgé yě bǐ píngshí guì yìxiē , érqiě
春节期间飞机票的价格也比平时贵一些，而且
yě yào tíqián yùdìng , cáinéng bǎozhèng mǎidào fēijīpiào . Yǒuxiē
也要提前预订，才能 保证 买到飞机票。有些
lùtú yuǎn , jīngjì tiáojiàn búcuò de rén , jiù xuǎnzé zuò fēijī
路途远、经济条件不错的人，就选择坐飞机
huíjiā guònián .
回家过年。

Chúle gōnggòng jiāotōng , chūnyùn háiyǒu yì zhī zhòngyào
除了 公共 交通，春运还有一支 重要
lìliang , jiùshì zìjiàchē . Xiànzài dàbùfen jiātíng dōu yǒule
力量，就是自驾车。现在大部分家庭都有了
qìchē , chūnyùn qījiān hěn duō rén xuǎnzé zìjǐ kāichē huíjiā .
汽车，春运期间很多人选择自己开车回家。
dàishàng jiārén , mǎi shàng lǐpǐn , jiàshǐzhe zìjǐ de qìchē
带上家人，买上礼品，驾驶着自己的汽车
huíjiā guònián . Yǒude kāichē yào sì-wǔ gè xiǎoshí , yǒude kāichē
回家过年。有的开车要四五个小时，有的开车
yào shí jǐ gè xiǎoshí huòzhě gèng cháng shíjiān . Chūnyùn qījiān ,
要十几个小时或者更 长 时间。春运期间，

gōnglù shang de chēliàng yě fēicháng mìjí , jíshǐ
公路上的车辆也非常密集(crowded)，即使
shì gāosù gōnglù yǒushí yě huì chūxiàn dǔchē de qíngkuàng , yìxiē
是高速公路有时也会出现堵车的情况，一些
zhòngyào de lùkǒu jiù huì gèng yōngdǔ .
重要的路口就会更拥堵(traffic jammed)。

Chūnyùn , shì Zhōngguó de yí dà tèsè . Jǐnguǎn nàshí
春运，是中国的一大特色。尽管那时
de jiāotōng hěn jǐnzhāng , dàn rénmen de xīnqíng shì qīdài de , shì
的交通很紧张，但人们的心情是期待的，是
gāoxìng de . Chúxī , quánjiārén zuò zài yìqǐ kàn chūnwǎn , chī
高兴的。除夕，全家人坐在一起看春晚[1]、吃
jiǎozi , lǚtú píláo jiù quánbù xiāoshī le , yíqiè huíjiā de
饺子，旅途疲劳就全部消失了，一切回家的
jīnglì dōu huì biànchéng xìngfú de huíyì .
经历都会变成幸福的回忆。

---

① Spring Festival TV Gala: It is a Chinese New Year special produced by China Central Television, with performances of arts, drama, dancing, singing and more. It has been part of the Chinese New Year celebration since the first CCTV Spring Festival Gala was launched in 1983. Every year since then, several million Chinese people gather in front of their television sets to watch the performances and await the coming of the lunar New Year.

Gōnggòng Jiāotōng : Fāngbiàn yòu Shíhuì
公共交通：方便又实惠

Zuìjìn Wú Bīng hěn gāoxìng, yīnwèi tā jiā fùjìn tōngle
最近吴冰很高兴，因为他家附近通了
dìtiě. Tā zài yì suǒ dàxué de túshūguǎn gōngzuò, yǐqián měi tiān
地铁。他在一所大学的图书馆工作，以前每天
zǎoshang yào zuò gōnggòng qìchē, zhōngjiān hái yào huàn yí cì
早上要坐公共汽车，中间还要换一次
chē, yào yí gè duō xiǎoshí cái néng dào gōngzuò dānwèi. Zǎoshang
车，要一个多小时才能到工作单位。早上
diǎn shàngbān, diǎn bàn zhīqián jiùyào chī wán zǎofàn,
8点上班，6点半之前就要吃完早饭，7
diǎn yǐqián zuò shàng gōngjiāochē. Xiànzài hǎo le, dìtiě cóng
点以前坐上公交车。现在好了，地铁从

jiā ménkǒu xiū dào dàxué ménkǒu, zhǐ xūyào duō fēnzhōng,
家门口修到大学门口，只需要20多分钟，

búyòng dānxīn dǔchē wèntí.
不用担心堵车问题。

Zài yìxiē dàchéngshì, dìtiě xiànlù yuèláiyuè duō, yě
在一些大城市，地铁线路越来越多，也

yuèláiyuè fāngbiàn. Zài Běijīng, sì huán yǐnèi píngjūn bùxíng
越来越方便。在北京，四环①以内平均步行

yì gōnglǐ, jiù kěyǐ dàodá yí gè dìtiězhàn. Dìtiě zhújiàn
一公里，就可以到达一个地铁站。地铁逐渐

xíngchéngle yí gè pángdà de wǎngluò, dàdà fāngbiànle
形成了一个庞大 (huge) 的网络，大大方便了

rénmen de shēnghuó, yě jiǎnqīngle dìmiàn shang de jiāotōng
人们的生活，也减轻了地面上的交通

yālì. Hěn duō chéngshì zhèxiē nián dōu tōngle dìtiě, lìrú
压力。很多城市这些年都通了地铁，例如

Sūzhōu, Shěnyáng, Chéngdū děngděng. Yóuyú Zhōngguó
苏州、沈阳、成都等等。由于中国

dìtiě de lìshǐ bú shì hěncháng, gè dà chéngshì de dìtiě shèbèi
地铁的历史不是很长，各大城市的地铁设备

dōu hěn xīn, chē zhàn xiū de dōu fēicháng piàoliang,
(facility) 都很新，车站修得都非常漂亮，

---

① The 4th Ring Road: Looking at a map of Beijing, we can see that there are multiple expressway roads which encircle the city, known as the "Ring Roads". The ring roads demarcate different areas within Beijing. From the center of the city radiating outward, there are the 2nd, 3rd, 4th, 5th, and 6th Ring Roads. The 4th Ring Road is around eight km from the center of Beijing.

yí zuòzuò dìtiězhàn , jiù hǎoxiàng yí dàodào dútè de fēngjǐngxiàn
一座座地铁站，就好像一道道独特的风景线
, xīyǐnzhe rénmen de mùguāng . Dìtiě gěi rénmen
(landscape)，吸引着人们的目光。地铁给人们
de shēnghuó dàiláile hěn dà fāngbiàn , xiànzài dìtiě xiū dào nǎli ,
的生活带来了很大方便，现在地铁修到哪里，
nǎli de fángzi jiù huì kuàisù de zhǎngjià .
哪里的房子就会快速地涨价。

Chūle dìtiězhàn , rénmen chángcháng xūyào zuò gōnggòng
出了地铁站，人们常常需要坐公共
qìchē . Wú Bīng fāxiàn , zhèxiē nián de gōnggòng qìchē yě
汽车。吴冰发现，这些年的公共汽车也
yuèláiyuè piàoliang le . Shǒuxiān gōnggòng qìchē dōu hěn xīn ,
越来越漂亮了。首先公共汽车都很新，
jīběn dōu shì zuìxīn de chēxíng . Qícì gōnggòng qìchē shang
基本都是最新的车型。其次公共汽车上
dōu ānzhuāngle kōngtiáo . Xiàjì wàimian yánrè , ér chē li què
都安装了空调。夏季外面炎热，而车里却
liángshuǎng yírén . Dōngtiān , wàimianfēichánghánlěng ,
凉爽宜人 (pleasant)。冬天，外面非常寒冷，
ér chē nèi yòu hěn wēnnuǎn . Lìngwài , xiànzài gōnggòng qìchē li hái
而车内又很温暖。另外，现在公共汽车里还
ānzhuāngle yídòng diànshì , zuò zài gōngjiāochē li , kěyǐ kànkan
安装了移动电视，坐在公交车里，可以看看
xīnwén , shēnghuó jìqiǎo děng diànshì jiémù . Wèile fāngbiàn
新闻、生活技巧等电视节目。为了方便
wàidìrén hé wàiguórén , gōngjiāochē nèi
外地人 (non-local resident) 和外国人，公交车内

hái yǒu Hànyǔ， Yīngyǔ liǎng zhǒng yǔyán bào zhànmíng， tóngshí
还有汉语、英语两种语言报站名，同时

háiyǒu diànzǐ xiǎnshìpái， xiǎnshì xià yí zhàn de míngchēng， zhèxiē
还有电子显示牌，显示下一站的名称，这些

dōushì yǐqián méiyǒu de. Xiànzài hěn duō chéngshì hái yǒule gōngjiāo
都是以前没有的。现在很多城市还有了公交

zhuānyòng chēdào， zài yídìng shíjiān nèi， biéde chēliàng bùxǔ
专用车道，在一定时间内，别的车辆不许

jìnrù， zhèyàng jiù bǎozhèngle gōngjiāochē de yùnxíng. Yīnwèi
进入，这样就保证了公交车的运行。因为

yí gè chéngshì yào xiǎng bù dǔchē， yīnggāi shǒuxiān fāzhǎn
一个城市要想不堵车，应该首先发展

gōnggòng jiāotōng， suǒyǐ zhèngfǔ yě chūtáile hěn duō gǔlì
公共交通，所以政府也出台了很多鼓励

zuò gōngjiāochē de cuòshī， ràng gōngjiāo biànde gèng fāngbiàn，
坐公交车的措施①，让公交变得更方便、

---

① The government of Beijing has enacted certain measurements to encourage more citizens to use public transportation in an effort to ease traffic congestion. The measurements include: issuing Beijing Municipal Administration Communication Cards (BMAC), developing the Beijing Bus Rapid Transit System, accelerating the building of the track transportation in the central city, and improving the bus lines etc.

gèng kuàijié
更快捷 (fast)。

Wú Bīng hái fāxiàn, zhèxiē nián gōngjiāochē de xiànlù duō
吴冰还发现，这些年公交车的线路多

le, hěn duō chē de xiànlù yě yáncháng le. Guòqù
了，很多车的线路也延长 (to extend) 了。过去

tā chūmén bànshì, chángcháng yào huàn hǎo jǐ cì chē, xiànzài
他出门办事，常常要换好几次车，现在

búyòng le, hěn duō dìfang dōu yǒule zhídá
不用了，很多地方都有了直达 (through, direct)

chē. Dìtiězhàn fùjìn chángcháng yǒu hǎo jǐ tiáo shènzhì shí duō
车。地铁站附近常常有好几条甚至十多

tiáo gōnggòng qìchē xiànlù, dào shìqū, jiāowài shènzhì gèng
条公共汽车线路，到市区、郊外甚至更

yuǎn, dōu kěyǐ búyòng huànchē.
远，都可以不用换车。

Jiāotōng gāofēng yìbān zài zǎochen diǎn dào diǎn,
交通高峰 (peak) 一般在早晨 7 点到 9 点，

xiàwǔ diǎn dào diǎn . Zhè duàn shíjiān shì rénmen shàngbān hé
下午5点到7点。这段时间是人们上班和

xiàbān bǐjiào jízhōng de shíjiān , zuòchē de rén hěn duō , gōnggòng
下班比较集中的时间，坐车的人很多，公共

qìchē jiù xiǎnde hěn jǐnzhāng , děng chē de rén duō , chēshang yě
汽车就显得很紧张，等车的人多，车上也

chángcháng méiyǒu zuòwèi . Bùguò duìyú nàxiē lǎoniánrén huòzhě
常常没有座位。不过对于那些老年人或者

háizi , yùnfù děng xūyào zhàogù de rén ,
孩子、孕妇 (pregnant woman) 等需要照顾的人，

dàjiā dōu néng zhǔdòng ràngzuò . Shòupiàoyuán yě jīngcháng
大家都能主动让座。售票员也经常

bāngzhù tāmen , tíxǐng niánqīngrén shǎozuò yíhuìr , jiāng zuòwèi
帮助他们，提醒年轻人少坐一会儿，将座位

ràng gěi xūyào de rén .
让给需要的人。

Chúle gōngjiāo , dìtiě zhīwài , Wú Bīng yǒushíhou yě
除了公交、地铁之外，吴冰有时候也

miǎnbuliǎo zuò chūzūchē . Gègè chéngshì de chūzūchē jiàgé bù
免不了坐出租车。各个城市的出租车价格不

yíyàng . Chūzūchēfèi yìbān fēnwéi gùdìng de qǐbùjià hé biàndòng
一样。出租车费一般分为固定的起步价和变动

de lǐchéngjià . Běijīng de jiē shang pǎozhe jǐ wàn liàng chūzū
的里程价。北京的街上跑着几万辆出租

qìchē , jīběn mǎnzúle shìmín chūxíng de xūyào . Chūzūchē de
汽车，基本满足了市民出行的需要。出租车的

jiàgé bú suàn tài guì , yìbān rén dōu chéngshòu de qǐ , suǒyǐ
价格不算太贵，一般人都承受得起，所以

zài Běijīng dǎ chē shì hěn píngcháng de shìqing . Chūzūchē sījī dōu
在北京打车是很平常的事情。出租车司机都

huì shuō yìxiē jiǎndān de Yīngyǔ , dàdà fāngbiànle wàiguó chéngkè ,
会说一些简单的英语，大大方便了外国乘客，

zhǐyào gàosu sījī mùdìdì , tāmen huì hěn shùnlì de dài chéngkè
只要告诉司机目的地，他们会很顺利地带乘客

dào nàli . Ér chéngkè zhǐ xūyào ànzhào jìjiàqì shang de jiàgé
到那里。而乘客只需要按照计价器上的价格

fù fèi jiù kěyǐ le , búyòng gěi sījī xiǎofèi .
付费就可以了，不用给司机小费。

Fēijī : Fēirù Xúncháng Bǎixìngjiā

飞机：飞入寻常百姓家

Lǎo Zhāng de érzi kǎoshàngle yì suǒ wàidì
老张的儿子考上了一所外地 (other places)
de dàxué , lí jiā yǒu liǎng qiān duō gōnglǐ . Érzi jiānchí yào zuò
的大学，离家有两千多公里。儿子坚持要坐
fēijī qù . Lǎo Zhāng shuō , zuò huǒchē jiù kěyǐ le , huǒchē
飞机去。老张说，坐火车就可以了，火车
piányi , érqiě zuò yìngzuò dehuà , hái
便宜，而且坐硬座 ([of trains] hard seat) 的话，还
kěyǐ bànjià . Běnlái kěyǐ zhǐ huā duō kuài qián , wèi shénme
可以半价。本来可以只花200多块钱，为什么
yào huā yìqiān duō ne ? Dàn Lǎo Zhāng de érzi bú zhème xiǎng ,
要花一千多呢？但老张的儿子不这么想，
duō gè xiǎoshí de huǒchē , búdàn hěn lèi , érqiě lù shang yě
20多个小时的火车，不但很累，而且路上也

hěn wúliáo, bùrú zuò fēijī, liǎng gè duō xiǎoshí jiù dào le,
很无聊，不如坐飞机，两个多小时就到了，

duō shūfu a. Zàishuō, jiāli yòu bú shì méi qián, kǎoshàng
多舒服啊。再说，家里又不是没钱，考上

dàxué yǐhòu, yì jiā rén qù Ōuzhōu lǚxíngle yí tàng, huāle hǎo
大学以后，一家人去欧洲旅行了一趟，花了好

jǐ wàn ne.
几万呢。

Lǎo Zhāng yě bú shì xīnténg qián, tā shì xiǎng
老张也不是心疼(to grudge)钱，他是想

ràng háizi dǒngdé yīnggāi jiéyuē, yīnggāi jiānkǔ fèndòu. Hòulái tā
让孩子懂得应该节约，应该艰苦奋斗。后来他

wèn le wèn háizi de tongxué, zhǐyào shì dào wàidì shàngxué de,
问了问孩子的同学，只要是到外地上学的，

yuǎn yìdiǎnr de dōu zuò fēijī. Lǎo Zhāng xiǎng, shídài jiùshì
远一点儿的都坐飞机。老张想，时代就是

bù yíyàng le, xiànzài lián háizi shàng dàxué dōu zuò fēijī.
不一样了，现在连孩子上大学都坐飞机。

Fēijī yǐjīng chéngle yìxiē rén chángyòng de chūxíng fāngshì.
飞机已经成了一些人常用的出行方式。

Qù hěn duō chéngshì lǚyóu, búlùn shì cānjiā lǚxíngshè háishi
去很多城市旅游，不论是参加旅行社还是

zìjǐ qù, dàduōshù rén dōu huì xuǎnzé fēijī. Fēijī de
自己去，大多数人都会选择飞机。飞机的

hǎochù búyòng duō shuō, fāngbiàn, shěngshí hái shūfu. Suǒyǐ,
好处不用多说，方便、省时还舒服。所以，

xiànzài jīchǎng rénshān-rénhǎi de, gēn guòqù de huǒchēzhàn
现在机场人山人海的，跟过去的火车站

chàbuduō. Xiǎngxiǎng duō nián qián, fēijī piàojià hěn guì,
差不多。想想20多年前，飞机票价很贵，

zhǐyǒu yǒuqiánrén huòzhě chūgōngchā de rén cái zuò. Érqiě zuòguo
只有有钱人或者出公差的人才坐。而且坐过

fēijī, háishi xiàng biéren xuànyào de zīběn
飞机，还是向别人炫耀(to flaunt)的资本(sth.

ne, hěn duō rén huì wèn
used to one's own advantage)呢，很多人会问

nǐ, zuò fēijī shénme gǎnshòu, wǎngxià kàn shì shénme gǎnjué,
你，坐飞机什么感受，往下看是什么感觉，

néng bu néng kàndào dì shang de qìchē, fángzi děngděng. Ér
能不能看到地上的汽车、房子等等。而

xiànzài, zuò fēijī gēn zuò huǒchē yíyàng, chéngle pǔtōng de
现在，坐飞机跟坐火车一样，成了普通的

jiāotōng gōngjù. Tànqīn, chūchāi,
交通工具。探亲、出差(be on a business trip)、

yuēhuì péngyou, hěn duō rén dōu xuǎnzé zuò fēijī. Zhōngguó
约会朋友，很多人都选择坐飞机。中国

miànjī hěn dà, liǎng dì zhījiān de jùlí yǒu de hěn yuǎn, zuò
面积很大，两地之间的距离有的很远，坐

fēijī yǐjīng bú shì shēnfèn dìwèi de xiàngzhēng, ér biànchéngle yì
飞机已经不是身份地位的象征，而变成了一

zhǒng pǔbiàn de chūxíng fāngshì.
种普遍的出行方式。

Gòumǎi fēijīpiào fēicháng fāngbiàn, zài chéngshì li yǒu hěn
购买飞机票非常方便，在城市里有很

duō fēijīpiào dàishòuchù, zǒu jǐ fēnzhōng, jiù kěyǐ zhǎodào yí
多飞机票代售处，走几分钟，就可以找到一

gè mài jīpiào de dìfang. Dāngrán nǐ hái kěyǐ dǎ diànhuà huòzhě zài
个卖机票的地方。当然你还可以打电话或者在

wǎngshang dìng jīpiào, yì-liǎng fēnzhōng jiù kěyǐ gǎodìng. Chúle
网上订机票，一两分钟就可以搞定。除了

mǎi piào, hái kěyǐ zài wǎngshang xuǎnzé zuòwèi, dǎyìn dēngjīpái
买票，还可以在网上选择座位、打印登机牌

, zuò zài jiā li, jiù bǎ zuòwèi xuǎnhǎo le.
(boarding check)，坐在家里，就把座位选好了。

Fēijīpiào jīngcháng dǎzhé , yǒushíhou
飞机票经常打折 (to have a discount)，有时候

fēijī piàojià gēn huǒchēpiào chàbuduō, yǒude shènzhì bǐ dòngchē
飞机票价跟火车票差不多，有的甚至比动车

hé gāotiě dōu piányi. Yìbān dǎ qī-bā zhé shì bǐjiào chángjiàn
和高铁都便宜。一般打七八折是比较常见

de, yě yǒu dǎ sān-sì zhé de shíhou. Dànshì dàole jié-jiàrì,
的，也有打三四折的时候。但是到了节假日、

hán-shǔjià děng wàngjì , piàojià chángcháng bù dǎzhé , zhè shíhou
寒暑假等旺季，票价常常不打折，这时候
jiù yào mǎi quánpiào le . Lǎo Zhāng
就要买全票 (buy full-price ticket) 了。老张
de érzi kāixué shì yùnshū wàngjì , jīpiào bù dǎzhé , jíshǐ shì
的儿子开学是运输旺季，机票不打折，即使是
xuésheng , yě méi shénme yōuhuì cuòshī .
学生，也没什么优惠措施。

Lǎo Zhāng de érzi yǐjīng bú shì dì-yī cì zuò fēijī le ,
老张的儿子已经不是第一次坐飞机了，
guòqù háizi fàng hán-shǔjià de shíhou , tāmen dōu huì dài háizi qù
过去孩子放寒暑假的时候，他们都会带孩子去
lǚyóu . Lǎo Zhāng de àirén zài dàxué li gōngzuò , měi nián yě yǒu
旅游。老张的爱人在大学里工作，每年也有
liǎng gè jiàqī , tāmen jiù lìyòng zhège jīhuì , dài háizi chūqu
两个假期，他们就利用这个机会，带孩子出去
lǚxíng . Yǒushíhou zài guónèi , yǒushíhou qù guówài . Tāmen lǚxíng
旅行。有时候在国内，有时候去国外。他们旅行

de mùdì， zhǔyào shì wèile kāikuò háizi de shìyě， péiyǎng
的目的，主要是为了开阔孩子的视野，培养

háizi duì shēnghuó de rè'ài hé duì měihǎo shìwù de xiàngwǎng.
孩子对生活的热爱和对美好事物的向往。

Qíshí Lǎo Zhāng hé àirén dàduōshù dìfang dōu le， wèile
其实老张和爱人大多数地方都去过了，为了

háizi， tāmen yuànyì zài qù yí cì， zhè gǎnjué gēn zìjǐ qù
孩子，他们愿意再去一次，这感觉跟自己去

yǒu hěn dà bùtóng.
有很大不同。

Dài háizi lǚyóu de jiātíng yǒu hěn duō. Chéngshì jiātíng li
带孩子旅游的家庭有很多。城市家庭里

zhǐyào jīngjì tiáojiàn yǔnxǔ， jiāzhǎng shì yuànyì bǎ qián huā zài háizi
只要经济条件允许，家长是愿意把钱花在孩子

shēn shang de. Zuò fēijī biànchéngle háizimen de jiācháng biànfàn
身上的。坐飞机便成了孩子们的家常便饭

. Suǒyǐ háizimen zǎojiù yǐjīng xíguànle
(common occurrence)。所以孩子们早就已经习惯了

zhèzhǒng chūxíng fāngshì. Bùjǐn shì háizimen， qíshí chéngrén
这种出行方式。不仅是孩子们，其实成人

yě yíyàng， rúguǒ wèile kuàijié， fāngbiàn yìbān dōu xuǎnzé fēijī
也一样，如果为了快捷、方便一般都选择飞机

chūxíng. Bùguò yě bù páichú lìwài， yǒude rén hàipà zuò fēijī，
出行。不过也不排除例外，有的人害怕坐飞机，

yǒude rén wèile xīnshǎng lǚtú de jǐngsè ér xuǎnzé zuò huǒchē.
有的人为了欣赏旅途的景色而选择坐火车。

suīrán zuò huǒchē xīnkǔ yìxiē， yǒushí xūyào zuò shàng jǐ tiān jǐ
虽然坐火车辛苦一些，有时需要坐上几天几

yè , dànqízhōng yě néng xiǎngshòu dào hěn duō lèqù .
夜，但其中也能 享受 到很多乐趣。

Búguò zài hěn duō nóngcūn , shānqū , zuò fēijī réngrán shì
不过在很多农村、山区，坐飞机仍然是
yí jiàn xīnxiānshì . Hěn duō lǎoniánrén yíbèizi
一件新鲜事。很 多老年人一辈子 (all one's life)
méiyǒu jīhuì zuò fēijī , shènzhì méiyǒu jiàn dàoguo tíng zài dìmiàn
没有机会坐飞机，甚至没有见到过停在地面
shang de fēijī . Tāmen zhǐnéng wàng zhe tiānkōng , kàn zhe
上 的飞机。他们只能 望 着 天空，看着
fēijī cóng gāochù fēi guòqu , zhǐ zhe nà xiǎoxiǎode , yínsè de
飞机从 高处飞过去，指着那小小的、银色的
fēixíngwù , shuō nà jiù shì fēijī . Tāmen yě zhǐnéngtīng nàxiē zuò
飞行物，说那就是飞机。他们也只能 听那些坐
guo fēijī de rén jiǎngjiang gǎnshòu , mǎnliǎn xiànmù de
过飞机的人 讲讲 感受，满脸 羡慕 (to envy) 的
biǎoqíng .
表情。

Xiànzài hěn duō dìfang dōu xīngjiàn le jīchǎng ,
现在 很 多地方都 兴建 (to build) 了 机场，
yóuqí shì yìxiē zhòngdiǎn lǚyóu chéngshì , jīběn dōu tōngle
尤其是一些 重点 旅游 城市，基本都通了

hángbān . Běijīng zé jiàn yǒu fēicháng piàoliang de hángzhàn
航班。北京则建有非常漂亮的T3航站

lóu , jīchǎng yě bǐ yuánlái dàle hǎo jǐ bèi . Shǒudū Jīchǎng yīnggāi
楼，机场也比原来大了好几倍。首都机场应该

shì Zhōngguó zuì fánmáng de jīchǎng . Měi tiān yǒu duō jiàcì
是中国最繁忙的机场。每天有1500多架次

qǐjiàng , měi tiān jìnchū de rénshù zài wàn rén zuǒyòu . Zài Chūn
起降、每天进出的人数在20万人左右。在春

Jié qījiān , hái huì gèng duō yìxiē .
节期间，还会更多一些。

Gāosù Gōnglù Gǎibiàn Shēnghuó
高速公路改变生活

Xiǎo Chén de yéye jīnnián kuài suì le, zhù zài nóngcūn.
小陈的爷爷今年快80岁了，住在农村。

Yīnwèi shēntǐ bú tài hǎo, měi gé liǎng gè yuè, jiù děi zuò chángtú
因为身体不太好，每隔两个月，就得坐长途

qìchē qù shěngchéng Zhèngzhōu
汽车去省城(provincial capital)——郑州

kànbìng. Cóng tā jiā dào Zhèngzhōu yào jìn wǔ gè xiǎoshí, chēzi
看病。从他家到郑州要近五个小时，车子

zǒngshì zǒuzǒu tíngtíng, zài jiāshàng niánlíng tài dà de guānxì,
总是走走停停，再加上年龄太大的关系，

Xiǎo Chén de yéye fēicháng nánshòu, yīnwèi hàipà zuòchē, duō cì
小陈的爷爷非常难受，因为害怕坐车，多次

shuō bú qù jiǎnchá le.
说不去检查(to examine)了。

nián, zhèzhǒng qíngkuàng fāshēngle gǎibiàn. Yì tiáo
2007年，这种情况发生了改变。一条
gāosù gōnglù jīngguò lǎojiā, kěyǐ zhíjiē dàodá shěngchéng.
高速公路经过老家，可以直接到达省城。
Yuánlái jìn wǔ gè xiǎoshí de chēchéng, xiànzài zǒu gāosù gōnglù zhǐ
原来近五个小时的车程，现在走高速公路只
xūyào yí gè bàn xiǎoshí. Zìcóng tōngle gāosù yǐhòu, qìchē
需要一个半小时。自从通了高速以后，汽车
biàndepíngwěn le, yéye zuò zài chēshang bú
变得平稳 (steady, smooth) 了，爷爷坐在车上不
nàme nánshòu le. Tā shènzhì shuō bú ràng jiārén péi, zìjǐ yí
那么难受了。他甚至说不让家人陪，自己一
gè rén qù shěngchéng dōu méi wèntí.
个人去省城都没问题。

Zhè tiáo gāosù gōnglù gěi yéye dàiláile fāngbiàn, yě gěi
这条高速公路给爷爷带来了方便，也给
Xiǎo Chén de fùqin dàiláile hǎochù. Xiǎo Chén de fùqin gǎo
小陈的父亲带来了好处。小陈的父亲搞

yǎngjīchǎng duō nián le , zuìjìn sān nián shì tā zuì kāixīn de
养鸡场 20 多年了，最近三年是他最开心的

sān nián , yīnwèi gāosù gōnglù tōngdàole jiā ménkǒu , tā de yùnshū
三年，因为高速公路通到了家门口，他的运输

chéngběn dàdà xiàjiàng le , zhuàn dào de qián yě duō le .
成本 (cost) 大大下降了，赚到的钱也多了。

gāosù gōnglù de kāitōng , ràng tā gāoxìngle hǎo jǐ gè yuè .
高速公路的开通，让他高兴了好几个月。

Xiǎo Chén yě yíyàng , tā dàxué bìyè hòu zài shěngchéng
小陈也一样，他大学毕业后在省城

gōngzuò . Guòqù huí tàng lǎojiā , shíjiān fēicháng jǐnzhāng , xiànzài
工作。过去回趟老家，时间非常紧张，现在

zé shì yí jiàn hěn qīngsōng de shìqing le . Tōngle gāosù gōnglù
则是一件很轻松的事情了。通了高速公路

yǐhòu , tā měi gè xīngqī dōu huì huí yí cì jiā , huíqù kànwàng
以后，他每个星期都会回一次家，回去看望

yéye , fùmǔ jí qítā qīnrén . Zhè tiáo gāosù gōnglù fāngbiànle
爷爷、父母及其他亲人。这条高速公路方便了

tā yì jiā sān dài de shēnghuó .
他一家三代的生活。

Cóng gāosù gōnglù dédào hǎochù de bù jǐnjǐn shì Xiǎo Chén
从高速公路得到好处的不仅仅是小陈

yì jiā . Gāosù gōnglù suǒ dào zhī chù , rénmen de shēnghuó fāngshì
一家。高速公路所到之处，人们的生活方式

yě zài qiāoqiāo fāshēng biànhuà . Shǎnxī Xī'ān dào Hànzhōng de
也在悄悄发生变化。陕西西安到汉中的

gāosù gōnglù , wéi chángqī fēngbì de shǎnnán gè dì kāibìle yì
高速公路，为长期封闭的陕南各地开辟了一

tiáo kuàisù tōngdào , yě lājìnle dāngdìrén yǔ wàijiè de jùlí .
条快速 通道，也拉近了当地人与外界的距离。

Zài Hànzhōng shìzhèngfǔ bùmén gōngzuò de Féng xiǎojiě , dǎsuàn
在 汉中 市政府部门 工作 的 冯小姐，打算

Chūnjié guòhòu yǔ nányǒu yìqǐ dào Xī'ān pāi jiéhūnzhào . Tā
春节 过后与男友一起到西安拍结婚照。她

shuō , yǐqián yóuyú jiāotōng búbiàn , gǎnjué shěnghuì Xī'ān shì
说，以前由于交通不便，感觉 省会 西安是

gè hěn yáoyuǎn de dìfang . Xī'ān dào Hànzhōng de gāosù gōnglù
个很 遥远 的地方。西安到 汉中 的高速公路

kāitōng hòu , xíngchē shíjiān cóng yuánlái de gè xiǎoshí suōduǎn dào
开通后，行车 时间从 原来的6个小时 缩短 到

gè xiǎoshí . Xiànzài Hànzhōngrén dào Xī'ān fāngbiàn le , gǎnjué
3个小时。现在 汉中人 到西安 方便 了，感觉

jùlí shang yě jìn le , suǒyǐ yě yuànyì dào Xī'ān bàn gè zhǒng
距离 上 也近了，所以也愿意到西安办各 种

shìqing le .
事情了。

Quèshí , gāosù gōnglù dàdà suōduǎnle yùnshū jùlí ,
确实，高速公路大大缩短了运输距离，

fāngbiànle rénmen de shēnghuó . "Yào xiǎng fù , xiān xiūlù ",
方便了人们的生活。"要想富，先修路①"，

zhè shì yí jù dàjiā fēicháng shúxī de kǒuhào , rán'ér
这是一句大家非常熟悉的口号(slogan)，然而

jiùshì zhè jù huà , shēngdòng de shuōmíngle gōnglù de yìyì hé
就是这句话，生动地说明了公路的意义和

zhòngyàoxìng . Zài Zhōngguó , Jīng- Jīn gāosù gōnglù jiànchéng
重要性。在中国，京津高速公路建成

tōngchē bú dào shí nián , cóng Běijīng dào Tiānjīn gè chū-rùkǒu
通车不到十年，从北京到天津11个出入口

fùjìn , xíngchéngle shí duō gè jīngjì jìshù kāifāqū
附近，形成了十多个经济技术开发区(develop-

, kāifā yòng dì miànjī yuē píngfāng gōnglǐ .
ment zone)，开发用地面积约70平方公里。

① Convenient traffic leads to opening business opportunities to distant or outlying areas.

Zhōngguó de gāosù gōnglù jiànshè, kāishǐ yú shìjì
中国的高速公路建设，开始于20世纪
niándài chūqī. nián, jiànchéngle Shànghǎi dào Jiādìng
80年代初期。1984年，建成了上海到嘉定
de dì-yī tiáo gāosù gōnglù. Suíhòu, yóuqí shì shìjì
的第一条高速公路。随后，尤其是20世纪90
niándài zhìjīn, gèdì dàguīmó de gāosù gōnglù jiànshè kāishǐ
年代至今，各地大规模的高速公路建设开始
lùxù zhǎnkāi. Gāosù gōnglù de jiànshè, búdàn gǎishànle gōnglù
陆续展开。高速公路的建设，不但改善了公路
de děngjí, gǎibiànle gōnglù shìyè de luòhòu miànmào, érqiě
的等级，改变了公路事业的落后面貌，而且
suōduǎnle tóng fādá guójiā zhījiān de chājù, yǒuxiào de lādòng
缩短了同发达国家之间的差距，有效地拉动
nèixū, cìjī le
内需 (domestic demand)，刺激 (to stimulate) 了
gāosù gōnglù fùjìn dìqū de jīngjì fāzhǎn hé fánróng.
高速公路附近地区的经济发展和繁荣 (flourshing)。

Sìtōng-bādá de gōnglù liánjiēzhe měi yí zuò chéngshì. Xiànzài
四通八达的公路连接着每一座城市。现在
měi gè xiāngzhèn yǐjí měi gè cūnzi zhījiān yě dōu xiūtōngle gōnglù.
每个乡镇以及每个村子之间也都修通了公路。
Yǐhòu, gāosù gōnglù huì yuèláiyuè duō, yuèláiyuè cháng.
以后，高速公路会越来越多，越来越长。
Gāosù gōnglù dàdà tígāole tōngxíng de sùdù, suōduǎnle yùnshū
高速公路大大提高了通行的速度，缩短了运输
shíjiān; gǎibiànle rénmen de shēnghuó.
时间；改变了人们的生活。

Zhōngguó Jìnrù Gāotiě Shídài

中国进入高铁时代

Zhōngguó zuì dà de liǎng gè chéngshì Běijīng hé Shànghǎi
中国 最大的两个 城市 ——北京和 上海
zhījiān tōngle gāosù tiělù , zhè ràng Liú Huān yì jiā rén fēicháng
之间通了高速铁路，这 让 刘 欢 一家人 非常
xīngfèn . Tāmen juédìng chéngzuò dì-yī tàng lièchē , tǐyàn gāotiě
兴奋。他们决定 乘坐 第一趟列车，体验高铁
dàilái de kuàilè . Wèicǐ , Liú Huān tíqián wǔ tiān jiù zài wǎngshang
带来的快乐。为此，刘 欢 提前五天就在 网上
yùdìngle huǒchēpiào . Xiànzài gāotiě zài Zhōngguó yǐjīng bú shì
预订了 火车票。现在高铁在 中国 已经不是

shénme xīnxiānshì le . nián, Běijīng dào Tiānjīn de gāotiě
什么新鲜事了。2008年，北京到天津的高铁

yǐjīng tōngchē, dàdà suōduǎnle liǎngdì zhījiān de jùlí ,
已经通车，大大缩短了两地之间的距离，130

duō gōnglǐ de jùlí , jǐnjǐn bàn gè xiǎoshí jiù dào le . Rán'ér,
多公里的距离，仅仅半个小时就到了。然而，

Běijīng dào Shànghǎi de gāotiě háishi gěi hěn duō rén dàiláile huānlè
北京到上海的高铁还是给很多人带来了欢乐

hé jīngxǐ .
和惊喜。

Liú Huān de àirén shì Shànghǎirén, měi dào jié-jiàrì ,
刘欢的爱人是上海人，每到节假日，

yì jiā rén jīngcháng huí Shànghǎi. Tā qīngchu de jìde duō nián
一家人经常回上海。他清楚地记得20多年

qián zuò huǒchē de tòngkǔ jīnglì . Nà shíhou huǒchē de sùdù hěn
前坐火车的痛苦经历。那时候火车的速度很

màn, dàgài měi xiǎoshí liù-qīshí gōnglǐ, cóng Běijīng dào Shànghǎi
慢，大概每小时六七十公里，从北京到上海

xūyào lái gè xiǎoshí . Shíjiān mànchánɡ bù shuō , chēpiào
需要20来个小时。时间漫长不说，车票
yě fēichánɡ nán mǎidào , chēxiānɡ lì fēichánɡ
也非常难买到，车厢(coach of train)里非常
yōnɡjǐ . Guòdào shanɡ , cèsuǒ li dàochù dōu shì rén , lián
拥挤。过道上、厕所里到处都是人，连
shànɡ-xiàchē dōu hěn kùnnan . Hòulái , huǒchē búduàn tísù ,
上下车都很困难。后来，火车不断提速，
měi xiǎoshí nénɡ dádào gōnɡlǐ zuǒyòu . Zài hòulái , yǒule
每小时能达到80公里左右。再后来，有了
dònɡchē , sùdù měi xiǎoshí nénɡ dádào duō
动车(bullet train)，速度每小时能达到100多
gōnɡlǐ . Xiànzài de gāosù tiělù měi xiǎoshí nénɡ dádào gōnɡlǐ
公里。现在的高速铁路每小时能达到300公里
zuǒyòu . Tài kuài le , cónɡ Běijīnɡ dào Shànɡhǎi , duō gōnɡlǐ
左右。太快了，从北京到上海，1500多公里

de lùchéng, zhǐ xūyào bú dào gè xiǎoshí. Érqiě zuò zài gāotiě
的路程，只需要不到5个小时。而且坐在高铁
chēxiāng li, gēn zuò zài fēijī shang shì de, zuòwèi fēicháng
车厢里，跟坐在飞机上似的，座位非常
shūfu, lièchēyuán de fúwù yě hěn zhōudào. Kànzhe lièchēyuán
舒服，列车员的服务也很周到。看着列车员
zhěngqí de fúzhuāng, wēixiào de miànróng, yí bù xiǎoxin huì
整齐的服装，微笑的面容，一不小心会
yǐwéi zìjǐ shì zài fēijī shang ne. Jīnnián Chūn Jié, Liú Huān
以为自己是在飞机上呢。今年春节，刘欢
dàizhe qīzi, háizi yìqǐ zuò gāotiě huí Shànghǎi, quán jiā
带着妻子、孩子一起坐高铁回上海，全家
rén dōu gāoxìng jíle.
人都高兴极了。

Gāosù tiělù bùjǐn gǎibiànle pǔtōngrén de shēnghuó, hái
高速铁路不仅改变了普通人的生活，还
lādòngle dāngdì de jīngjì. Suízhe Wǔhàn dào Guǎngzhōu gāotiě de
拉动了当地的经济。随着武汉到广州高铁的
kāitōng, fēichí de huǒchē bǎ Guǎngzhōu, Chángshā, Wǔhàn děng
开通，飞驰的火车把广州、长沙、武汉等
chéngshì jǐnmì lián zài yìqǐ, ràng zhèxiē dìqū de jīngjì biànde
城市紧密连在一起，让这些地区的经济变得
shífēn huóyuè, yìxiē qǐyè yě bǎ gōngchǎng zhuǎnyí dào kāitōng
十分活跃，一些企业也把工厂转移到开通
gāotiě de dìfang. Suízhe shíkōng jùlí de lājìn, Guǎngdōng,
高铁的地方。随着时空距离的拉近，广东、
Húnán, Húběi sān shěng zài rényuán, zījīn, xìnxī děng
湖南、湖北三省在人员、资金、信息等

fāngmiàn de jiāoliú gèngjiā pínfán , zīyuán yōuhuà
方面的交流更加频繁(frequently)，资源优化

jìn yí bù jiāsù , xíngchéngle yí
(optimize)进一步加速(speed up)，形成了一

gègè xīn de jīngjì zēngzhǎngdiǎn , zhèxiē jīngjì zēngcháng
个个新的经济增长点，这些经济增长

diǎn dàidòng zhōubiān dìqū chǎnyè fāzhǎn , zuìzhōng shíxiàn zhěnggè
点带动周边地区产业发展，最终实现整个

dìqū de jīngjì zēngzhǎng .
地区的经济增长。

Qián jǐ nián , rénmen hěn xiànmù chūguó de rén , tīng tāmen jiǎng
前几年，人们很羡慕出国的人，听他们讲

hěn duō xīnqí de jīnglì , qízhōng jiù yǒu gāosù tiělù . Bǐrú
很多新奇的经历，其中就有高速铁路。比如

Rìběn de xīngànxiàn , Fǎguó , Déguó de gāosù lièchē děng .
日本的新干线，法国、德国的高速列车等。

Xiànzài Zhōngguó yě yǒule zhèyàng de tiělù , hěn duō rén dōu xiǎng
现在中国也有了这样的铁路，很多人都想

zuòzuo gāotiě , shènzhì bùshǎo wàiguórén yě xiǎng zuòzuo Zhōngguó
坐坐高铁，甚至不少外国人也想坐坐中国

de gāotiě . Gāosù tiělù yǐjīng chéngle Zhōngguó de xiàngzhēng ,
的高铁。高速铁路已经成了中国的象征，

ānquán , shūshì , kuàijié , gěi rénmen dàilái yuèláiyuè duō de
安全、舒适、快捷，给人们带来越来越多的

fāngbiàn . Xiànzài hěn duō dà chéng shì zhījiān dōu zài jiànshè gāosù
方便。现在很多大城市之间都在建设高速

tiělù , yòngbuliǎo duō jiǔ , gāosù tiělù jiù huì xiàng yì zhāng
铁路，用不了多久，高速铁路就会像一张

dàwǎng yíyàng pūkāi , suíbiàn qù nǎr , dōu fēicháng fāngbiàn .
大网一样铺开，随便去哪儿，都非常方便。

Suízhe yì tiáotiáo gāotiě de kāitōng , lǎobǎixìng gǎnshòu dào de zuì
随着一条条高铁的开通，老百姓感受到的最

dà hǎochù kěnéng jiùshì mǎi piào búyòng fāchóu le . Yóuyú gāotiě
大好处可能就是买票不用发愁了。由于高铁

shì gōngjiāohuà yùnxíng , yì tiān yǒu shí jǐ tàng shènzhì jǐ shí tàng
是公交化运行，一天有十几趟甚至几十趟

bāncì , kěyǐ suí dào suí mǎi huǒchēpiào . Dāngrán , gāotiě de
班次，可以随到随买火车票。当然，高铁的

piàojià bǐ pǔtōng lièchē , dòngchē de guì yìxiē , yìxiē rén kǎolǜ
票价比普通列车、动车的贵一些，一些人考虑

dào jīngjì yīnsù , réngrán xuǎnzé pǔtōng huǒchē huòzhě dòngchē .
到经济因素，仍然选择普通火车或者动车。

Búguò , gāosù tiělù de kuàisù fāzhǎn yě yǐnqǐle rénmen
不过，高速铁路的快速发展也引起了人们

de dānyōu . Lìrú : gāotiě shì bú shì yuè kuài yuè hǎo , Ānquán
的担忧。例如：高铁是不是越快越好，安全

zěnme bǎozhàng , Fúwù zěnyàng jiāqiáng děngděng .
怎么 保障 (to ensure)，服务 怎样 加强 等等 。

Yǒuguān bùmén zhèngzài kǎolǜ zhèxiē yìjiàn , bǎ ānquán fàng zài
有关 部门 正在 考虑这些意见，把安全放在

dì-yī wèi . Xiànzài gāosù lièchē de sùdù yǐjīng jiàngle bùshǎo ,
第一位。现在高速列车的速度已经降了不少，

rénmen búzài zhuīqiú juéduì sùdù . Gāosù tiělù de jiànshè sùdù
人们不再追求绝对速度。高速铁路的建设速度

yě fàngmànle yìxiē , zhòngdiǎn háishì yào bǎozhàng gōngchéng de
也放慢了一些， 重点 还是要 保障 工程 的

zhìliàng . Gāosù tiělù de jiànshè yīnggāi zhúbù fāzhǎn , ér bú shì
质量。高速铁路的建设 应该逐步发展，而不是

kěyǐ yí yè wánchéng de .
可以一夜 完成 的。

Gōngjiāo Yìkǎtōng Bùjǐnjǐn Shì Gōngjiāokǎ

公交一卡通①：不仅仅是公交卡

Lǎo Zhāng shēnghuó zài Hángzhōu, gōngzuò dānwèi
老张生活在杭州，工作单位
lí jiā hěn yuǎn, tā měi tiān yào zuò wǔ zhàn dìtiě, xiàle
离家很远，他每天要坐五站地铁，下了
dìtiě, hái yào zuò jǐ zhàn gōngjiāochē. Yǐqián, mǎi piào
地铁，还要坐几站公交车。以前，买票
hěn máfan, zuò dìtiě yào páiduì mǎi piào,
很麻烦 (troublesome)，坐地铁要排队买票，
gōngjiāochē shang ren hěn duō, yǒushíhou lí shòupiàoyuán hěn
公交车上人很多，有时候离售票员很
yuǎn, xūyào bǎ qián ràng rén chuán lái chuán qù de.
远，需要把钱让人传 (pass on) 来传去的。
Zhè jǐ nián qíngkuàng bù yíyàng le, gōngjiāo gōngsī fāxíngle
这几年情况不一样了，公交公司发行了
"gōngjiāo yìkǎtōng", shàngchē zhǐyào shuā kǎ jiù kěyǐ le,
"公交一卡通"，上车只要刷卡就可以了，

---

① Public Transportation Card: It is a smart card for public transportation and related uses. With these cards time is not wasted on buying a ticket, checking the ticket, and then paying for the ticket. They also eliminate one of the needs for carrying cash and can help commuters avoid taking small change. Many cities in China have issued this kind of card: in some cities, the card is not only used for taking public transportation, but also for shopping. Certain cards may be used across cities for added convenience.

dìtiě hé gōngjiāochē dōu kěyǐ tōngyòng . Qiánmén shàngchē ,
地铁和公交车都可以通用。前门上车，
hòumén xiàchē , zhèyàng dàjiā yě jiù dōu zìjué
后门下车，这样大家也就都自觉 (on one's
páiduì le , tā juéde zìcóng yòngle gōngjiāokǎ yǐhòu ,
initiative) 排队了，他觉得自从用了公交卡以后，
shàng xià chē de zhìxù yě hǎo duō le , jǐnguǎn rén háishi
上下车的秩序 (order) 也好多了，尽管人还是
hěn duō , dàn hǎoxiàng bú nàme yōngjǐ le .
很多，但好像不那么拥挤了。

Lǎo Zhāng jīngcháng dào Shànghǎi chūchāi , zuò chūzūchē fù
老张经常到上海出差，坐出租车付
fèi shí , sījī zǒngshì wèn : " Shuā kǎ háishi
费时，司机总是问："刷卡 (pay by card) 还是
xiànjīn ? " Shuā kǎ dāngrán shì zhǐ gōngjiāo yìkǎtōng . " Dǎ chē
现金？" 刷卡当然是指公交一卡通。"打车

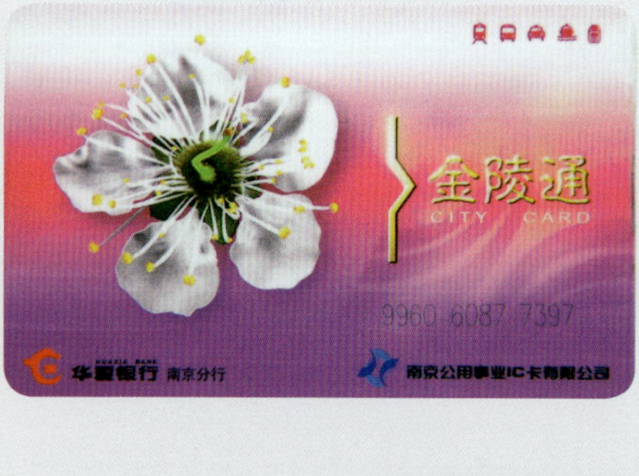

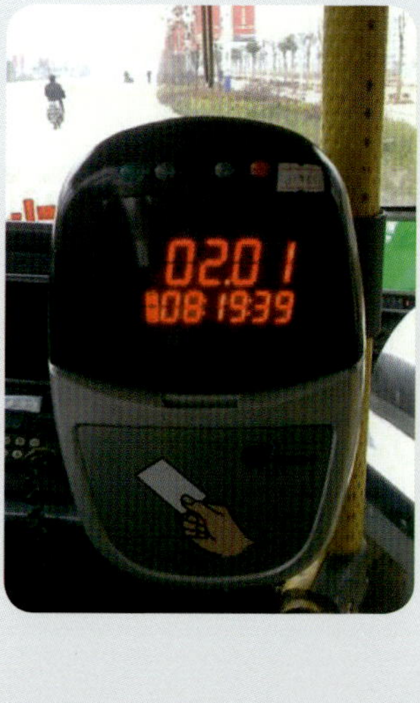

yě kěyǐ shuā zhè zhāng kǎ ma？” Kāishǐ de shíhou Lǎo Zhāng
也可以刷这张卡吗？”开始的时候老张
hái yǐwéi shì shuā yínhángkǎ， ér sījī shīfu shuō：“ Búshì
还以为是刷银行卡，而司机师傅说：“不是
yínhángkǎ， shì gōngjiāokǎ。” Xiànzài chūzūchē gōngsī gēn gōngjiāo
银行卡，是公交卡。”现在出租车公司跟公交
xìtǒng shì liánwǎng de， kěyǐ yòng gōngjiāokǎ lái fù
系统是联网 (network) 的，可以用公交卡来付
chūzūchēfèi。
出租车费。

Zhèxiē nián hěn duō chéngshì dōu zài tuīguǎng gōngjiāo yìkǎtōng，
这些年很多城市都在推广公交一卡通，
bǎ gōngjiāo yìkǎtōng zuòwéi fùfèi shǒuduàn zhī yì。 Zài bùtóng
把公交一卡通作为付费手段之一。在不同
chéngshì， gōngjiāo yìkǎtōng chúle chéngzuò jiāotōng gōngjù
城市，公交一卡通除了乘坐交通工具
wài， qí gōngnéng yě yǒu bùtóng。 Shànghǎi de yìkǎtōng bùjǐn
外，其功能也有不同。上海的一卡通不仅
kěyǐ zài gōnggòng qìchē、 dìtiě shang xiāofèi， yě yǐjīng jìnrù
可以在公共汽车、地铁上消费，也已经进入
chūzūchē lǐngyù。 Zài Hángzhōu， kěyǐ yòng yìkǎtōng bōdǎ
出租车领域。在杭州，可以用一卡通拨打
gōngyòng diànhuà， hái kěyǐ dào bùfen shāngdiàn、 chāoshì、
公用电话，还可以到部分商店、超市、
xībǐngwū、 cāntīng、 yàodiàn、 diànyǐngyuàn děng shuā kǎ xiāofèi。
西饼屋、餐厅、药店、电影院等刷卡消费。
Jiānglái kěyǐ shǐyòng gōngjiāo yìkǎtōng shuā kǎ xiāofèi de shāngdiàn
将来可以使用公交一卡通刷卡消费的商店

huì yuèláiyuè duō. Bùjǐn
会越来越多。不仅

rúcǐ, jiānglái Zhèjiāng Shěng
如此，将来浙江省

suǒyǒu gāosù gōnglù yě kě
所有高速公路也可

shuā yìkǎtōng jiāofèi tōngguò,
刷一卡通交费通过，

wèile gǔlì
为了鼓励 (to encourage)

sījī xíngchéng shuā kǎ xíguàn,
司机形成刷卡习惯，

kāishǐ huì yǒu yídìng de yōuhuì. Tóngshí, shǒujī shuā kǎ de cèshì
开始会有一定的优惠。同时，手机刷卡的测试

yě yǐjīng jiéshù, yòng suíshēn xiédài de shǒujī jiù kě
也已经结束，用随身携带 (carry on) 的手机就可

qīngsōng shuā kǎ chéngzuò dìtiě, gōngjiāo. Gōngyuán niánpiào
轻松刷卡乘坐地铁、公交。公园年票①

yě yǐjīng gēn gōngjiāo yìkǎtōng hé èr wéi yī, quánmiàn shíxiànle
也已经跟公交一卡通合二为一，全面实现了

diànzǐhuà. Jīnhòu, yìkǎtōng de gōngnéng jiāng huì yuèláiyuè
电子化。今后，一卡通的功能将会越来越

duō, jīhū kěyǐ fùgài suǒyǒu de rìcháng zhīfù,
多，几乎可以覆盖 (to cover) 所有的日常支付，

jùshuō jiānglái kěyǐ gēn yínháng liánwǎng, qí zuòyòng kěyǐ
据说将来可以跟银行联网，其作用可以

---

① Parks annual pass: A type of smart card issued by the government. After purchasing the parks annual pass, unlimited access is granted to most parks in a given city.

xiāngdāngyú yì zhāngxìnyòngkǎ huòzhě chǔxùkǎ . Dàoshíhou , jiāo
相当于一张信用卡或者储蓄卡。到时候，交

diànfèi , méiqìfèi , wùyèfèi děng , yě kěyǐ shǐyòng yìkǎtōng .
电费、煤气费、物业费等，也可以使用一卡通。

yìkǎtōng de gōngnéng zhème duō le , rénmen yě jiù bù xūyào tài
一卡通的功能这么多了，人们也就不需要太

duō de kǎ le . Yì zhāng yìkǎtōng , suǒyǒu de fùfèi wèntí dōu
多的卡了。一张一卡通，所有的付费问题都

jiějué le .
解决了。

Rúguǒ xiǎng gěi yìkǎtōng chōngzhí , yě hěnfāngbiàn , hěnduō
如果想给一卡通充值，也很方便，很多

gōngjiāo chēzhàn , dìtiězhàn dōu kěyǐ . Dàn xiànzài de gōngjiāo
公交车站、地铁站都可以。但现在的公交

yìkǎtōng hái bú shì shímíngzhì , shàngmian méiyǒu míngzi hé gèrén
一卡通还不是实名制，上面没有名字和个人

xìnxī， yě méiyǒu mìmǎ， rúguǒ diūshī dehuà， hěn kěnéng jiù
信息，也没有密码，如果丢失的话，很可能就
zhǎobudào le， suǒyǐ yào bǎoguǎn hǎo.
找不到了，所以要保管好。

Mùqián， Hángzhōu de jiāotōng yìkǎtōng fāxíngliàng hái zài
目前，杭州的交通一卡通发行量还在
búduàn zēngjiā. Suízhe dìtiě xiànlù yuèláiyuè cháng， fàqiǎ
不断增加。随着地铁线路越来越长，发卡
shùliàng huì yuèláiyuè duō. Xiànzài， fánshì yǒu qīnqi， péngyou
数量会越来越多。现在，凡是有亲戚、朋友
lái Hángzhōu lǚxíng， Lǎo Zhāng dōu bāngzhe mǎi yì zhāng
来杭州旅行，老张都帮着买一张
yìkǎtōng. Tā juéde zhè zhāng xiǎo kǎpiàn de zuòyòng tài dà le，
一卡通。他觉得这张小卡片的作用太大了，
yǒule tā， jiù shì bú dài qiánbāo yě méiguānxi le.
有了它，就是不带钱包也没关系了。

Ràng Rén Dǔxīn de Dǔchē

让人堵心的堵车

Xiǎo Xiè de jiā lí shìzhōngxīn bǐjiào yuǎn, dàgài yǒu duō
小谢的家离市中心比较远，大概有 30 多
gōnglǐ, tā měi tiān kāichē shàng-xiàbān. Qùnián Xiǎo Xiè kāichē dào
公里，他每天开车上下班。去年小谢开车到
gōngsī, xūyào yígè xiǎoshí; dàole jīnnián niándǐ, zhìshǎo yào
公司，需要一个小时；到了今年年底，至少要
huā xiǎoshí fēnzhōng. Yuányīn shì tā zhù de xiǎoqū sījiāchē
花 1 小时 20 分钟。原因是他住的小区私家车
yuèláiyuè duō, yǒude yì jiā yǒu liǎng liàng qìchē
(private car) 越来越多，有的一家有两辆汽车
le. Yǒushíhou qìchē méi chū xiǎoqū, jiù yǐjīng bèi dǔzhù le,
了。有时候汽车没出小区，就已经被堵住了，

lù shang de qíngkuàng jiù gèng kěyǐ
路上的情况就更可以
xiǎngxiàng le , dǔchē ràng tā yuèláiyuè
想象了，堵车让他越来越
fánnǎo .
烦恼。

Bùjǐnjǐn shì Xiǎo Xiè wèi dǔchē
不仅仅是小谢为堵车
fánnǎo , Lǎo Liú yě shì zhèyàng . Tā de
烦恼，老刘也是这样。他的
jiā lí gōngzuò dānwèi bú tài yuǎn , rúguǒ
家离工作单位不太远，如果
bù dǔchē dehuà , zuò gōngjiāochē
不堵车的话，坐公交车20
duō fēnzhōng jiù néng dào . Dàn Lǎo Liú
多分钟就能到。但老刘
měitiān xiàwǔ diǎn xiàbān shí , dōu xiān
每天下午6点下班时，都先
bù huíjiā . Tā shuō : “ Xiànzài huíqu
不回家。他说：“现在回去
hé diǎn huíqu , dàojiā de shíjiān
和7点回去，到家的时间
chàbuduō . ” diǎn zuǒyòu zhèngshì zuì
差不多。”6点左右正是最
dǔchē de shíhou , yǒushíhou děng chē
堵车的时候，有时候等车
jiù xūyào duō fēnzhōng . Píngshí
就需要20多分钟。平时

jǐ fēnzhōng yí tàng de chē, dàole gāofēngqī, zǒng bèi dǔ zài lù
几分钟一趟的车，到了高峰期，总被堵在路

shang, bàntiān yě kàn bu dào lái yí liàng. Lù shang zǒuzǒutíngtíng,
上，半天也看不到来一辆。路上走走停停，

yí gè hónglǜdēng wǎngwǎng yào děng jǐ fēnzhōng, cóng zuò shàng chē
一个红绿灯往往要等几分钟，从坐上车

dào jiā, wǎngwǎng yào yí gè xiǎoshí. Lǎo Liú shuō, bùrú qí
到家，往往要一个小时。老刘说，不如骑

zìxíngchē kuài. Suǒyǐ rúguǒ zháojí huíjiā, tā jiù qí zìxíngchē.
自行车快。所以如果着急回家，他就骑自行车。

Měidào jiérì, dǔchē wèntí jiù gèng yánzhòng le. Shǒuxiān,
每到节日，堵车问题就更严重了。首先，

jié-jiàrì suǒyǒu wěi hào de qìchē dōu kěyǐ shànglù, bú zài
节假日所有尾号的汽车都可以上路，不再

xiànxíng . Qícì , jié-jiàrì hěn duō rén dōu yào chūmén bànshì ,
限行①。其次，节假日很多人都要出门办事，
huòzhě dài háizi qù gōngyuán , děngděng . Dì-sān , rúguǒ
或者带孩子去公园，等等。第三，如果
jié-jiàrì shíjiān bǐjiào cháng , hái huì yǒu hěn duō wàidì de chēliàng
节假日时间比较长，还会有很多外地的车辆
hé yóukè dàolái . Yǒu yì nián Zhōngqiūjié , yì cháng xiǎoyǔ
和游客到来。有一年中秋节，一场小雨
gèng shì ràng Běijīng xiànrù le dà dǔchē , yōngdǔ lùduàn
更是让北京陷入 (fall into) 了大堵车，拥堵路段
chāoguò tiáo , quánchéng de chēliàng dōu zài yìdiǎnr yìdiǎnr
超过 140 条，全城的车辆都在一点儿一点儿
de nuódòng , zuò zài chē li de rén yě hěn wúnài .
地挪动 (move slowly)，坐在车里的人也很无奈。

Xiànzài shìjiè shang hěn duō chéngshì dōu duōduōshǎoshǎo cúnzài
现在世界上很多城市都多多少少存在
dǔchē wèntí . Zhōngguó de qíngkuàng yě chàbuduō , rúguǒ
堵车问题。中国的情况也差不多，如果
gǎnshàng jiāotōng gāofēng , huòzhě guāfēng xiàyǔ děng tiānqì , lù
赶上交通高峰，或者刮风下雨等天气，路

① Traffic restriction: A traffic regulation used for easing the traffic congestion. In 2007, Beijing began to introduce traffic restrictions by adopting odd-even license plate restrictions on alternative days to reduce congestion and pollution. The restriction took effect during the Beijing Olympic period. Cars with numbered license plates ending with odd numbers were restricted one day and the next day cars with numbered license plates ending with even numbers were restricted. Later, the measurement developed to the Weekly No-Driving Day regulations where Beijing's car owners are prohibited from driving one day each week according to the last number of their license plates. Currently, the regulation is in effect in Beijing. Several other cities in China have similar traffic restriction measures.

shang jiù huì biànde gèng dǔ , yí gè lùkǒu děngshàng wǔ fēnzhōng
上就会变得更堵，一个路口等上五分钟

shènzhì gèng cháng shíjiān yě shì chángyǒu de . Mùqián , Zhōngguó
甚至更长时间也是常有的。目前，中国

dàduōshù chéngshì bùtóng chéngdù de cúnzàizhe jiāotōng yōngdǔ
大多数城市不同程度地存在着交通拥堵

xiànxiàng . Gēnjù tǒngjì , quán guó gè chéngshì
现象。根据统计(statistics)，全国667个城市

zhōng , yuē yǒu sān fēn zhī èr de chéngshì zài jiāotōng gāofēng shí
中，约有三分之二的城市在交通高峰时

jīdòngchē chēsù xiàjiàng , chūxiàn yōngdǔ , dà-zhōng chéngshì gèng
机动车车速下降，出现拥堵，大中城市更

yánzhòng . Zài yìxiē dàchéngshì shìqū , jīdòngchē píngjūn shísù
严重。在一些大城市市区，机动车平均时速

yǐjīng xiàjiàngdào gōnglǐ, Ér zài shìzhōngxīn, jīdòngchē shísù
已经下降到12公里，而在市中心，机动车时速
gèng shì zhǐyǒu dào gōnglǐ. Pǔtōng zìxíngchē de shísù wéi
更是只有8到10公里。普通自行车的时速为15
gōnglǐ zuǒyòu, zài zhèzhǒng qíngkuàng xià, kāichē bùrú qíchē
公里左右，在这种情况下，开车不如骑车
kuài, yǐjīng bù shì gè xiàohuà, érshì shēnghuó zhōng de zhēnshí
快，已经不是个笑话，而是生活中的真实
yí mù.
一幕。

Yì tiān bàngwǎn, chūzūchē sījī Lǎo Wáng bèi dǔ
一天傍晚(nightfall)，出租车司机老王被堵
zài yí zuòqiáo xià, Tā xiàchē yí kàn, qiánhòu zuǒyòu dōu shì chē.
在一座桥下，他下车一看，前后左右都是车。
Qiánmian mǐ chù, shì yí gè shízì lùkǒu, fēnzhōng
前面30米处，是一个十字路口，15分钟
hòu, Lǎo Wáng réng zài yuándì. Tā dǎkāi yì bāo yān, mànmān
后，老王仍在原地。他打开一包烟，慢慢
chōu qǐlai. Lǎo Wáng shuō: "Měi tiān pǎo gè xiǎoshí, dǔchē
抽起来。老王说："每天跑8个小时，堵车
yě děi liǎng-sān gè xiǎoshí." Jiāotōng dēng hóngle yòu lǜ, lǜle
也得两三个小时。"交通灯红了又绿，绿了
yòu hóng, rán'ér chē jiùshì bú dòng. Zài tā kànlái, jíshǐ shì
又红，然而车就是不动。在他看来，即使是
"xiànxíng", yě bù néng jiějué dǔchē de wèntí, yīnwèi hěn duō
"限行"，也不能解决堵车的问题，因为很多
jiātíng dōu yǒu liǎngliàngchē, kěyǐ huànzhe kāi.
家庭都有两辆车，可以换着开。

Gè dàchéngshì dōu zài xiǎng bànfǎ zhìlǐ
各大城市都在想办法治理(bring under control)堵车的问题，其中最有效的办法，就是大力发展公共交通，减少私家车出行的数量。相信经过一段时间，堵车现象会得到缓解(ease up)。

dǔchē de wèntí, qízhōng zuì yǒuxiào de bànfǎ, jiùshì dàlì fāzhǎn gōnggòng jiāotōng, jiǎnshǎo sījiāchē chūxíng de shùliàng. Xiāngxìn jīngguò yí duàn shíjiān, dǔchē xiànxiàng huì dédào huǎnjiě

Chángtúchē Kāidào Jiāménkǒu

长途车开到家门口

Yīnwèi lǎojiā zài wàidì de yuángù, Hóng Mín jīngcháng zuò
因为老家在外地的缘故，洪民经常坐

chángtúchē huíjiā. Tā de lǎojiā lí Běijīng duō gōnglǐ, zuò
长途车回家。他的老家离北京300多公里，坐

chángtú qìchē xūyào sì-wǔ gè xiǎoshí.
长途汽车需要四五个小时。

Bùguǎn zài nǎ zuò chéngshì, chángtú qìchēzhàn shì bùkě
不管在哪座城市，长途汽车站是不可

shǎo de, érqiě hěn duō chéngshì bùzhǐ yí gè chángtú chēzhàn.
少的，而且很多城市不只一个长途车站。

Chángtúchē dàbùfen shì kāiwǎng jiāoqū huòzhě zhōubiān dìqū de .
长途车大部分是开往郊区或者周边地区的。

Dànshì zhè jǐ nián , hěn duō chéngshì zhījiān yě fāzhǎn qǐle chángtú
但是这几年，很多城市之间也发展起了长途

yùnshū , yǒude xūyào pǎo duō gè xiǎoshí cái néng dào .
运输，有的需要跑20多个小时才能到。

Hóng Mín de lǎojiā lí Běijīng suàn shì bǐjiào jìn de .
洪民的老家离北京算是比较近的。

Chángtúchē xūyào zǒu liǎng duàn lù , yíduàn shì gāosù gōnglù ,
长途车需要走两段路，一段是高速公路，

yíduàn shì pǔtōng gōnglù , dàyuē fēnbié xūyào liǎng gè xiǎoshí de
一段是普通公路，大约分别需要两个小时的

chēchéng . Xiànzài zuò chángtúchē fēicháng fāngbiàn , cóng Běijīng
车程。现在坐长途车非常方便，从北京

dào tā de lǎojiā , yì tiān yǒu shí lái tàng chē . Cóng zǎochen
到他的老家，一天有十来趟车。从早晨6

diǎn dào xiàwǔ diǎn , chàbuduō yí gè xiǎoshí jiù huì fā yí tàng
点到下午4点，差不多一个小时就会发一趟

chē . HóngMín bǐjiào xǐhuan zuò zǎochen de chē , yīnwèi zǎochen bù
车。洪民比较喜欢坐早晨的车，因为早晨不

dǔchē , cóng zuò shàng chē dào xiàchē , sì gè xiǎoshí jiù dàodá
堵车，从坐上车到下车，四个小时就到达

lǎojiā . Zài cūnkǒu de gōnglù biān xiàchē , zài bùxíng fēnzhōng
老家。在村口的公路边下车，再步行10分钟

jiù dàojiā le . Zuò chángtú qìchē bǐ zuò huǒchē hái yào fāngbiàn ,
就到家了。坐长途汽车比坐火车还要方便，

yīnwèi huǒchē yào xiān zuòdào xiànchéng , xiànchéng
因为火车要先坐到县城 (county town)，县城

lí lǎojiā háiyǒu gōnglǐ lù, zhè duàn lù háiyào zuò qìchē

离老家还有30公里路，这段路还要坐汽车

huòzhě dǎ chē. Zuò chángtú qìchē kěyǐ zhíjiē dào jiā ménkǒu,

或者打车。坐长途汽车可以直接到家门口，

suǒyǐ gèng fāngbiàn yìxiē.

所以更方便一些。

Chángtúchē shang píngshí rén búsuàn duō, gè zuòwèi de chē

长途车上平时人不算多，40个座位的车

yě jiù bàn chē rén, yǒushí shènzhì hái bú dào gè. Chángtúchē

也就半车人，有时甚至还不到20个。长途车

hěn shūfu, zuòwèi kěyǐ tiáojié, duōshù shíhou tā

很舒服，座位可以调节 (to adjust)，多数时候他

shàngchē jiù shuìjiào. Yí jiào xǐng lái

上车就睡觉。一觉醒来 (wake up after a sound

, chàbuduō yě jiù kuài dào jiā le. Yǒushíhou tā yě gēn

sleep)，差不多也就快到家了。有时候他也跟

zhōuwéi de rén liáoliaotiānr, shuōshuo zài Běijīng de gùshi. Rúguǒ

周围的人聊聊天儿，说说在北京的故事。如果

gǎnshàng zhōumò huò jié-jiàrì, zuòwèi jiù huì jǐnzhāng yìxiē,

赶上周末或节假日，座位就会紧张一些，

bìxū tíqián dàodá qìchēzhàn, cái néng mǎi dào piào. Érqiě
必须提前到达汽车站，才能买到票。而且

nà shíhou hěn duō chángtúchē jiù bú àn zhèngdiǎn
那时候很多长途车就不按正点 (on schedule)

fāchē le, zhǐyào màiwánle piào, shàng mǎnle rén, jiù huì chūfā.
发车了，只要卖完了票，上满了人，就会出发。

Rén duō de shíhou, shòupiào dàtīng huì jǐ de mǎnmǎn de.
人多的时候，售票大厅会挤得满满的。

Rúguǒ chē shang chéngkè bù duō, yě kěyǐ zài zhōngtú
如果车上乘客不多，也可以在中途

shàngchē. Sījī huòzhě shòupiàoyuán dōu yǒu míngpiàn,
上车。司机或者售票员都有名片，

shàngmian xiězhe tāmen de diànhuà. Chéngkè zhǐyào dǎ yí gè
上面写着他们的电话。乘客只要打一个

diànhuà, shuōmíng zài qìchē jīngguò de mǒu gè dìfang děnghòu,
电话，说明在汽车经过的某个地方等候，

tāmen jiù huì zài nàli tíngchē, ér búbì qù qìchēzhàn. Dāngrán
他们就会在那里停车，而不必去汽车站。当然

qiántí shì chéngkè yīnggāi tíqián dàodá nàli, qìchē shì bú huì zài
前提是乘客应该提前到达那里，汽车是不会在

nàli tíngzhe děng de. Rúguǒ zài qìchēzhàn yǐjīng shàng mǎnle rén,
那里停着等的。如果在汽车站已经上满了人，

zhōngtú jiù bú huì tíngchē.
中途就不会停车。

Xiànzài jiāotōng jǐngchá duìyú chāoyuán
现在交通警察对于超员 (be overmanned)

jiǎnchá de hěn yángé, yí liàng qìchē yīnggāi zuò duōshao rén, jiù
检查得很严格，一辆汽车应该坐多少人，就

zhǐnéng zuò duōshao rén, bù néng chāoguò guīdìng de shùliàng,
只能 坐 多少 人，不能 超过 规定的 数量，
fǒuzé jiùyào shòudào chǔfá. Chúle fákuǎn yǐwài, háiyào jiāng
否则就要 受到 处罚。除了罚款以外，还要将
duōyú de rén xiè xiàlai, ānpái chéngzuò qítā chēliàng. Yīnwèi
多余的人卸下来，安排 乘坐 其他 车辆。因为
zhè jǐ nián suízhe qìchē shùliàng de zēngjiā, jiāotōng shìgù yǒu
这几年随着汽车 数量 的增加，交通 事故有
yídìng chéngdù de shàngshēng, suǒyǐ bìxū kòngzhì chángtú kèchē
一定 程度的 上升 ，所以必须控制 长途客车
chāoyuán de wèntí, cóng gēnběn shang èzhì jiāotōng
超员 的问题，从 根本 上 遏制 (to curb) 交通
shìgù, bǎohù rénmín de shēngmìng hé cáichǎn ānquán. Duìyú zhè
事故，保护人民的 生命 和财产 安全。对于这
yì diǎn chéngkè hé sījī shì dōu nénggòu lǐjiě de.
一 点 乘客 和司机是都 能够 理解的。

Děng chángtúchē xiàle gāosù gōnglù, chéngkè suíshí kěyǐ
等 长途车 下了高速公路，乘客 随时可以
xuǎnzé jiùjìn de dìfang xiàchē, zhè shì zuò chángtú qìchē zuì fāngbiàn
选择就近的地方下车，这是坐 长途汽车最 方便
de dìfang. Chángtú qìchē yántú jīngguò hěn duō cūnzhuāng,
的地方。长途 汽车 沿途 经过 很 多 村庄 ，
chéngkè kěyǐ zài cūnkǒu zhíjiē xiàchē.
乘客 可以在村口直接下车。

Zuò chángtú qìchē shàng cèsuǒ shì gè wèntí. Sījī yìbān huì
坐 长途汽车 上 厕所是个问题。司机一般会
kǎolǜ dào chéngkè de shēnglǐ xūyào, liǎng-sān
考虑到 乘客 的 生理 (physiological) 需要， 两三

gè xiǎoshí yǐhòu， tā huì zài jiāyóuzhàn huòzhě fúwùqū
个小时以后，他会在加油站或者服务区(service

tíngchē， qǐng dàjiā xiàchē shàng cèsuǒ. Dàn rúguǒ chéngkè
area)停车，请大家下车上厕所。但如果乘客

quèshí hěn zháojí， yě kěyǐ qǐngqiú sījī zài fùjìn yǒu cèsuǒ de
确实很着急，也可以请求司机在附近有厕所的

dìfang tíngchē. Yóuyú chángtúchē yùnxíng shíjiān cháng， zài jiā
地方停车。由于长途车运行时间长，再加

shàng yǒu rén zài chángtúchē shang chī dōngxi， qìwèi bù róngyì
上有人在长途车上吃东西，气味不容易

sànfā chūqu， suǒyǐ chē nèi de kōngqì yǒushíhou bú tài hǎo.
散发出去，所以车内的空气有时候不太好。

Xiànzài hěn duō chángtúchē biànde hěn háohuá， yǒu
现在很多长途车变得很豪华(deluxe)，有

hěn duō shuāngcéng háohuá wòpù chángtú qìchē.
很多双层豪华卧铺(sleeper)长途汽车。

Zhèzhǒng chē xiàng huǒchē yíyàng， kěyǐ tǎng zài shàngmian
这种车像火车一样，可以躺在上面

shuìjiào . Chángtúchē shang háiyǒu yǐngxiàng shèbèi ,
睡觉。长途车上还有DVD影像设备，
sījī huì bōfàng yìxiē lùxiàng gěi chéngkè guānkàn . Rúguǒ tiānqì
司机会播放一些录像给乘客观看。如果天气
lěng huò rè , sījī hái huì dǎkāi kōngtiáo , ràng chéngkè gèng
冷或热，司机还会打开空调，让乘客更
shūshì yìxiē .
舒适一些。

Suízhe jiāotōng yùnshūyè de fāzhǎn , chángtú qìchē biànde
随着交通运输业的发展，长途汽车变得
yuèláiyuè shūshì , ānquán . Tā yǔ huǒchē , fēijī yìqǐ ,
越来越舒适、安全。它与火车、飞机一起，
gòuchéngle yùnshū de zhòngyào zǔchéng bùfen . Yǒude rén fàngqì
构成了运输的重要组成部分。有的人放弃
huǒchē ér xuǎnzé jīngcháng zuò chángtú qìchē le .
(give up) 火车而选择经常坐长途汽车了。
Chángtú qìchē de piàojià bǐ huǒchē lüè guì yìxiē . Dàn xiāngbǐ
长途汽车的票价比火车略贵一些。但相比
huǒchē , fāchē shíjiān , shàng-xiàchē dìdiǎn děng gèng línghuó .
火车，发车时间、上下车地点等更灵活。

Zìjiàyóu : Suíxīn'érdòng
自驾游：随心而动

Guóqìng Jié qián, yí gè zài Qīngdǎo de péngyou dǎ lái diànhuà, shuō tā yào zài shí yuè yī rì jiéhūn, xīwàng wǒ hé nǚyǒu néng qù cānjiā tāmen de hūnlǐ. Zhènghǎo, qián bùjiǔ wǒ gāng mǎile yí liàng qìchē, wǒ xiǎng, zhè cì wǒ kěyǐ hé xīn'ài de nǚyǒu lái gè chángtú lǚxíng le.

国庆节前，一个在青岛的朋友打来电话，说他要在十月一日结婚，希望我和女友能去参加他们的婚礼(wedding)。正好，前不久我刚买了一辆汽车，我想，这次我可以和心爱的女友来个长途旅行了。

Chūfā qián , wǒ shǒuxiān jiǎnchále xūyào dài de dōngxi ,
出发前，我首先检查了需要带的东西，
bāokuò shēnfènzhèng , xìnyòngkǎ děngděng , ránhòu jiǎnchále
包括身份证、信用卡等等，然后检查了
qìchē yǒu méiyǒu shénme máobing . Ér nǚyǒu què zuì guānxīn
汽车有没有什么毛病。而女友却最关心
shēnghuó wèntí , tā bùjǐn dàile língshí , shuǐguǒ , hái dàile
生活问题，她不仅带了零食、水果，还带了
fángshàishuāng shénme de . Tā bǎ zhèxiē dōngxi
防晒霜 (sunscreen) 什么的。她把这些东西
yǒutiáo-yǒulǐ de bǎifàng zài chēxiāng nèi , ránhòu gāogāo-xìngxìng de
有条有理地摆放在车厢内，然后高高兴兴地
zuò zài fùjiàshǐ de wèizhì shang , xiàozheshuō :
坐在副驾驶 (second driver) 的位置上，笑着说：
“ Kāi ba , wǒmen de mèngxiǎng zài yuǎnfāng . ”
“开吧，我们的梦想在远方。”

Yí lù shang , wǒ péi nǚyǒu liáozhe tiān , gěi tā jiǎng gùshi ,
一路上，我陪女友聊着天，给她讲故事、
jiǎng xiàohuà , ǒu’ěr wǒmen yě tíng zài lùbiān xiūxi xiūxi , huǎnjiě
讲笑话，偶尔我们也停在路边休息休息，缓解
yíxià lǚtú de píláo . Jīngguò yì tiān de chángtú lǚxíng , wǒmen
一下旅途的疲劳。经过一天的长途旅行，我们
zhōngyú dàodále měilì de hǎibīng chéngshì Qīngdǎo . Cānjiā
终于到达了美丽的海滨城市——青岛。参加
wán péngyou de hūnlǐ , wǒmen jiàchē láidàole xiàngwǎng yǐ jiǔ
完朋友的婚礼，我们驾车来到了向往已久
de dàhǎi biān . Wǒmen gāoxìng de dǎkāile chēmén , zǒushàngle
的大海边。我们高兴地打开了车门，走上了

sōngruǎn de hǎitān , ránhòu zuò zài hǎibiān de yánshí
松软的海滩(beach)，然后坐在海边的岩石(rock)
shang， yìbiān tīngzhe zhènzhèn tāo shēng， yìbiān kànzhe tiānshang
上，一边听着阵阵涛声，一边看着天上
de xīngxing， wǒmen gǎnjué xìngfú jíle .
的星星，我们感觉幸福极了。

Zìjǐ kāichē qù lǚyóu， bèi chēngwéi " zìjiàyóu
自己开车去旅游，被称为“自驾游(self-
". Suízhe yuèláiyuè duō de jiātíng mǎile qìchē，
driving travel)”。随着越来越多的家庭买了汽车，
zìjiàyóu yě jiù yuèláiyuè liúxíng. Yì jiā rén kāichē qù hěn yuǎn
自驾游也就越来越流行。一家人开车去很远
de dìfang lǚxíng， hùxiāng guānxīn， hùxiāng zhàogù， yìqǐ kàn
的地方旅行，互相关心、互相照顾，一起看

shān， kàn hǎi， jìshì yì zhǒng fàngsōng， yě zēngjìnle jiātíng
山、看海，既是一种放松，也增进了家庭

chéngyuán de gǎnqíng. Xiànzài， hěn duō jiātíng jiébàn
成员的感情。现在，很多家庭结伴(go with)

zìjiàyóu， jǐ liàng chē， shí jǐ liàng chē yìqǐ， kāi dào mǒu
自驾游，几辆车、十几辆车一起，开到某

gè dìfang. Zhèzhǒng fāngshì yǐjīng chéngwéi dà-zhōng chéngshì lǐ
个地方。这种方式已经成为大中城市里

zhōng-qīngniánrén， shènzhì lǎoniánrén suǒ rè'ài de lǚyóu fāngshì.
中青年人、甚至老年人所热爱的旅游方式。

Zìjiàchē de tuántǐ dàduō shì zìfā zǔzhī
自驾车的团体大多是自发(spontaneous)组织

de， cānjiāzhě dàduō yǐ jiātíng huò qīnpéng wéi dānwèi. Yǒude shì
的，参加者大多以家庭或亲朋为单位。有的是

tóngshì， tóngxué guānxì， yǒude shì qīnqi péngyou guānxì， tāmen
同事、同学关系，有的是亲戚朋友关系，他们

yuánlái dōu rènshi， guānxì yě búcuò， yuànyì zài yìqǐ huódòng.
原来都认识，关系也不错，愿意在一起活动。

Mǒu yì jiā tíchū xiǎngfǎ hòu， jiù liánxì dàjiā， hěn kuài kěyǐ
某一家提出想法后，就联系大家，很快可以

zǔchéng yí gè zìjiàyóu tuántǐ. Lín xiānsheng jiùshì zhème yí
组成一个自驾游团体。林先生就是这么一

gè rèxīnrén， tā fēicháng xǐhuan zìjiàyóu， chángcháng juéde
个热心人，他非常喜欢自驾游，常常觉得

yí gè rén chūqu méi yìsi， suǒyǐ tā jīngcháng zǔzhī tuántǐ
一个人出去没意思，所以他经常组织团体

zìjiàyóu huódòng. Qùnián Chūnjié qījiān， tā lìyòng tiān
自驾游活动。去年春节期间，他利用7天

jiàqī， zǔzhīle yí cì tóngxué zìjiàyóu. Tā fādòng dàxué
假期，组织了一次同学自驾游。他发动大学

tóngxué zhōng yǒuchē de jiātíng， yǐ jiātíng wéi dānwèi， dàjiā yìqǐ
同学中有车的家庭，以家庭为单位，大家一起

kāichē qù Guǎngxī. Yígòng yǒu gè jiātíng cānjiāle nà cì
开车去广西。一共有15个家庭参加了那次

huódòng， yí lù shang， chēduì hàohào-dàngdàng
活动，一路上，车队浩浩荡荡(in formidable

， fēicháng qìpài， tíng xiàlai xiūxi de shíhou， dàjiā
array)，非常气派，停下来休息的时候，大家

shuōshuō-xiàoxiào， ràng tā xiǎngqǐ shàng dàxué de shíhou， dàjiā
说说笑笑，让他想起上大学的时候，大家

hùxiāng bāngzhù， tuánjié yǒu'ài de qíngjǐng， zìjiàyóu díquè
互相帮助，团结友爱的情景，自驾游的确

qǐdàole zēngjìn gǎnqíng de zuòyòng， érqiě bǐ mǒu yì jiā dāndú
起到了增进感情的作用，而且比某一家单独

chūqu yào yǒuyìsi de duō.
出去要有意思得多。

Yě yǒude zìjiàyóu tuántǐ shì zài wǎngshang zǔzhī de, tāmen
也有的自驾游团体是在网上组织的，他们

yuánlái bìng bù rènshi, ér zhǐshì xiǎngdào mǒu yí gè gòngtóng
原来并不认识，而只是想到某一个共同

de dìfang lǚyóu. Zhèyàng tōngguò wǎngzhàn, qún děng,
的地方旅游。这样通过网站、QQ群等，

tāmen jiù jiànlìle liánluò, zǔchéng línshí de tuántǐ. Zěnyàng shǐ
他们就建立了联络，组成临时的团体。怎样使

lǚyóu guòchéng dádào wánměi shì tāmen tèbié guānzhù de wèntí.
旅游过程达到完美是他们特别关注的问题。

Zìjiàyóu zuì dānxīn de jiùshì lùchéng ānpái hé shíjiān wèntí,
自驾游最担心的就是路程安排和时间问题，

rúguǒ duì lùchéng bù shúxī, nàme hěn kěnéng dānwu xíngchéng
如果对路程不熟悉，那么很可能耽误行程

, suǒyǐ chūyóu zhīqián zuìhǎo xiān xiǎng hǎo lùxiàn ,
(journey)，所以出游之前最好先 想 好路线，

ānpái hǎoshíjiān .
安排好时间。

Hái yǒude shì lǚxíngshè zǔzhī de zìjiàyóu . Lǚxíngshè tōngguò
还有的是旅行社组织的自驾游。旅行社 通过

guǎnggào , xuānchuán , gàosu dàjiā yào qù nǎli , rúhé
广告、 宣传 ，告诉大家要去哪里，如何

zǔchéng zìjiàyóu tuántǐ děngděng , yǒu chē de rén kěyǐ bàomíng
组成 自驾游团体 等等 ，有车的人可以 报名

cānjiā . Zài zhèzhǒng qíngkuàng xià , dàduōshù lǚxíngshè wèi
参加。在 这种 情况 下，大多数旅行社为

zìjiàchē lǚyóuzhě tígōng dìngfáng , dìngcān jí qìchē wéixiū
自驾车旅游者提供订房、订餐及汽车维修

děng jīběn fúwù , ér bù néng tígōng chēliàng ràng
(maintenance) 等基本服务，而不能提供车辆 让

yóukè zìjǐ jiàshǐ . Yìxiē qìchē jùlèbù yě zǔzhī qí
游客自己驾驶。一些汽车俱乐部 (club) 也组织其

huìyuánjìnxíng zìjiàyóu huódòng, bìngzài zìjiàyóu guòchéng zhōng
会员进行自驾游活动，并在自驾游过程中

wèi huìyuán tígōng wéixiū, jiùyuán jí xiànlù zhǐyǐn, shísù yúlè
为会员提供维修、救援及线路指引、食宿娱乐

děng yǒuguān fúwù .
等有关服务。

Yǒuxiē zìjiàchē tuántǐ shì wèile tànxiǎn, xúnqiú gèng dà
有些自驾车团体是为了探险，寻求更大

de cìjī . Xiànzài Zhōngguó bùjǐn liúxíng kāi zìjǐ de chēqù
的刺激。现在中国不仅流行开自己的车去

lǚyóu, hái xīngqǐle yìdì zūchē lǚyóu, yě jiùshì zuò fēijī
旅游，还兴起了异地租车旅游，也就是坐飞机

dàomǒu yí gè dìfang hòu, zài dāngdì zū yí liàng chē, ránhòu kāizhe
到某一个地方后，在当地租一辆车，然后开着

qù zhōubiān dìqū yóulǎn . Zhèyàng zuò bùjǐn
去周边 (surrounding) 地区游览。这样做不仅

jiéyuēle chéngběn, gèng shǐ yìdì
节约了成本，更使异地 (places away from home)

zìjiàyóu chéngwéi kěnéng .
自驾游成为可能。

Zìxíngchē de Mìngyùn
自行车的命运

Zài Zhōngguó hěn duō chéngshì, qí zìxíngchē de rén yuèláiyuè
在中国很多城市，骑自行车的人越来越

shǎo le. Yìxiē yuánlái hěn kuān de zìxíngchēdào, yóuyú
少了。一些原来很宽的自行车道，由于

méiyǒu duōshǎo zìxíngchē, ér bèi huàfēn chū yì tiáo
没有多少自行车，而被划分 (mark off) 出一条

jīdòngchēdào, shǐdé zìxíngchēdào yě biànde yuèláiyuè zhǎi le.
机动车道，使得自行车道也变得越来越窄了。

Díquè, bǐqǐ kāi qìchē lái, qí zìxíngchē yòu lèi yòu màn.
的确，比起开汽车来，骑自行车又累又慢。

Lǐ Dé jīnnián kuài suì le, tā yìzhí jiānchí qí zìxíngchē. Tā
李德今年快50岁了，他一直坚持骑自行车。他

cóng jiā dào gōngsī, yào qí bàn gè duō xiǎoshí. Tā juéde qíchē
从家到公司，要骑半个多小时。他觉得骑车

jì huánbǎo yòu kěyǐ duànliàn shēntǐ. Búguò tā qīzi què shuō:
既环保又可以锻炼身体。不过他妻子却说：

"Bié qíchē le, mǎi liàng qìchē ba. Xiàtiān nàme rè, dōngtiān
"别骑车了，买辆汽车吧。夏天那么热，冬天

nàme lěng, qí zìxíngchē duō xīnkǔ a." Qí zìxíngchē shì tǐng
那么冷，骑自行车多辛苦啊。"骑自行车是挺

xīnkǔ de, guādàfēng de shíhou, qí bu dòng, zhǐhǎo tuīzhe zǒu.
辛苦的，刮大风的时候，骑不动，只好推着走。

Gǎnshàng xià dàyǔ, huì lín shī quánshēn, yí fù
赶上下大雨，会淋湿 (get drenched) 全身，一副

lángbèibùkān de yàngzi.
狼狈不堪 (in an extremely awkward position) 的样子。

Suízhe zhèxiē nián jīngjì de fāzhǎn, hěn duō jiātíng dōumǎile qìchē.
随着这些年经济的发展，很多家庭都买了汽车。

Qí zìxíngchē shàng-xiàbān de rén shǎole hěn duō. Lǐ Dé juéde,
骑自行车上下班的人少了很多。李德觉得，

xiànzài qí zìxíngchē méiyǒu yǐqián shūfu le. Shǒuxiān lù shang de
现在骑自行车没有以前舒服了。首先路上的

qìchē tài duō, yǒuxiē lùkǒu, qìchē, zìxíngchē dōuyào jīngguò,
汽车太多，有些路口，汽车、自行车都要经过，

bú tài ānquán. Gōnggòng qìchē kàobiān de shíhou, jīngcháng
不太安全。公共汽车靠边的时候，经常

yǐngxiǎng dào qí zìxíngchē de rén, yě hěn róngyì fāshēng shìgù.
影响到骑自行车的人，也很容易发生事故。

Qícì, diàndòngchē yuèláiyuè duō, diàndòngchē sùdù hěn kuài,
其次，电动车越来越多，电动车速度很快，

gēn pǔtōng zìxíngchē zài yìqǐ, yě róngyì fāshēng pèngzhuàng
跟普通自行车在一起，也容易发生碰撞

. Dì-sān, guòtiānqiáo, dìxià tōngdào bù fāngbiàn,
(collision)。第三，过天桥、地下通道不方便，

yóuqí shì shàngtiānqiáo de shíhou, bùdébù shǐjìn xiàngshàng tuī,
尤其是上天桥的时候，不得不使劲向上推，

fēicháng xīnkǔ. Dì-sì, zìxíngchē tíngchē yě chéngle wèntí,
非常辛苦。第四，自行车停车也成了问题，

guòqù yǒu hěn duō cún zìxíngchē de dìfang, xiànzài zhèzhǒng dìfang
过去有很多存自行车的地方，现在这种地方

yuèláiyuè bù hǎo zhǎo le. Hěn duō lóu qián bú ràng tíng, yàofàng
越来越不好找了。很多楼前不让停，要放

dào hěn yuǎn de dìfang huòzhě shì dìxiàshì qù.
到很远的地方或者是地下室去。

Lìngwài, diàndòng zìxíngchē zài hěn dà chéngdù shang yǐjīng
另外，电动自行车在很大程度上已经

qǔdàile pǔtōng de zìxíngchē.
取代了普通的自行车。

Yí wèi suì de Shànghǎirén
一位50岁的上海人

shuō: "Zuìchū, wǒ xuǎnzé
说："最初，我选择

diàndòng zìxíngchē shì yīnwèi
电动自行车是因为

bù néng rěnshòu mótuōchē de
不能忍受摩托车的

qìyóuwèi, dànshì yí duàn
汽油味，但是一段

shíjiān zhīhòu， wǒ yìshi
时间之后，我意识

dào diàndòng zìxíngchē bǐ
到电动自行车比

mótuōchē gèng ānquán， gèng
摩托车更安全、更

huánbǎo. Diàndòng zìxíngchē
环保。电动自行车

de jiàgé bú tài guì， wánquán
的价格不太贵，完全

kěyǐ jiēshòu.” Diàndòng zìxíngchē chéngle hěn duō shìmín de
可以接受。”电动自行车成了很多市民的

zuì ài， yóuqí shì yìxiē kuàidì gōngsī de yuángōng，
最爱，尤其是一些快递公司(courier)的员工，

tāmen bǎ huòwù fàng zài hòumian， jiāng tāmen yùnsòng dào chéngshì
他们把货物放在后面，将它们运送到城市

de měi yí gè jiǎoluò. Màidāngláo hé Kěndéjī de kuàidìyuán yě
的每一个角落。麦当劳和肯德基的快递员也

huì qízhe diàndòng zìxíngchē， jiāng zhuāng yǒu hànbǎobāo hé
会骑着电动自行车，将装有汉堡包和

zhájīròu de hézi sòngdào zhǐdìng de dìdiǎn. Diàndòng zìxíngchē
炸鸡肉的盒子送到指定的地点。电动自行车

hái shòudàole wàiguó duǎnqī lǚxíngzhě hé liúxuéshēng de huānyíng.
还受到了外国短期旅行者和留学生的欢迎。

Tāmen dào Zhōngguó hòu， mǎi liàng diàndòngchē， jiù kěyǐ zài
他们到中国后，买辆电动车，就可以在

zhège chéngshì zìyóu-zìzài de xíngshǐ le. Yóuqí shì nàxiē xǐhuan
这个城市自由自在地行驶了。尤其是那些喜欢

guānguāng de péngyou, kěyǐ qízhe tā, dàodá chéngshì de měi
观光的朋友，可以骑着它，到达城市的每
gè jiǎoluò, tǐhuì biéyǒu yìfān fēngwèi de fēngsú mínqíng.
个角落，体会别有一番风味的风俗民情。

Bù jǐnjǐn zài chéngshì, jíshǐ zài nóngcūn, xiànzài
不仅仅在城市，即使在农村，现在
diàndòngchē yě hěn pǔjí le. Zài Héběi Shěng de yí gè cūnzi,
电动车也很普及了。在河北省的一个村子，
jīhū jiājiā dōu yǒu liǎng-sān liàng diàndòngchē, hěn shǎo yǒu rén qí
几乎家家都有两三辆电动车，很少有人骑
pǔtōng de zìxíngchē le.
普通的自行车了。

Dànshì diàndòng zìxíngchē yě cúnzài ānquán wèntí. Tāmen
但是电动自行车也存在安全问题。它们
xíngshǐ zài fēijīdòngchēdào, yǔ pǔtōng zìxíngchē děng róngyì fāshēng
行驶在非机动车道，与普通自行车等容易发生
pèngzhuàng. Lìngwài yóuyú diàndòng zìxíngchē sùdù hěn kuài,
碰撞。另外由于电动自行车速度很快，
zài guǎiwān shí, yě róngyì hé jīdòngchē, xíngrén děng fāshēng
在拐弯时，也容易和机动车、行人等发生
pèngzhuàng. Yīncǐ yóu diàndòng zìxíngchē yǐnfā de chēhuò yě
碰撞。因此由电动自行车引发的车祸也
yuèláiyuè duō.
越来越多。

Hěn duō rén rènwéi, chéngshì rúguǒ fàngqìle zìxíngchē shì jiàn
很多人认为，城市如果放弃了自行车是件
fēicháng kěxī de shìqing. Yīnwèi zìxíngchē bù xiāohào néngyuán,
非常可惜的事情。因为自行车不消耗能源，

méiyǒu wūrǎn, hěn huánbǎo, suǒyǐ jiànyì chéngshì yīnggāi dàlì
没有污染，很环保，所以建议城市应该大力

fāzhǎn zìxíngchē zūlìn fúwù. Bǐrú, Běijīng Shì
发展自行车租赁 (to rent) 服务。比如，北京市

shèzhì gè zuǒyòu zìxíngchē zūlìndiǎn, xíngchéng wàn liàng
设置 1000 个左右自行车租赁点， 形成 5 万辆

yǐshàng zūlìn guīmó. Rán'ér shíjì qíngkuàng què bú lèguān.
以上租赁规模。然而实际情况却不乐观。

Suízhe gōnggòng jiāotōng yuèláiyuè fāngbiàn, zūlìn zìxíngchē
随着公共交通越来越方便，租赁自行车

de rén bìng bù duō. Yí gè xiǎo shāngdiàn de lǎobǎn shuō, zài
的人并不多。一个小商店的老板说，在

bù yuǎnchù céng yǒu yí gè zìxíngchē zūlìndiǎn, duō shì yóukè
不远处曾有一个自行车租赁点，多是游客

zūjiè . Hòulái zūchē de rén yuèláiyuè shǎo , gōngsī zhuàn bu dào
租借。后来租车的人越来越少，公司 赚 不到
qián , zǎo zài yì nián qián jiù bǎ zìxíngchē dōu chè zǒu le . Wèile
钱，早在一年 前就把自行车都撤走了。为了
jiějué zìxíngchē zūlìn shìchǎng de wèntí , Běijīng xiǎng le hěn duō
解决自行车租赁 市场 的问题，北京 想 了很 多
bànfǎ . Jiāotōng bùmén zhèngzài xiǎng bànfǎ huīfù zìxíngchēdào ,
办法。交通 部门 正在 想 办法恢复自行车道，
quèbǎo zìxíngchēdào tōngchàng . Lìng yì fāngmiàn , duìyú qīnzhàn
确保自行车道 通畅 。另 一 方面 ，对于 侵占
zìxíngchēdào de xíngwéi yào yánlì jìnzhǐ , duìyú zìxíngchēdào yǔ
自行车道的行为要严厉禁止，对于自行车道与
jīdòngchēdào chōngtū de dìfang , huì jǐn kěnéng shíxiàn dàolù fēnlí ,
机动车道 冲突的地方，会尽可能实现道路分离，
bǎozhàng zìxíngchē chūxíng de ānquán chàngtōng .
保障 自行车 出行 的 安全 畅通 (unblocked)。
Lìngwài zhǔnbèi tuīxíng zìxíngchē yōuxiān xíngshǐ . Zài chéngshì
另外 准备 推行 自行车 优先 行驶。在 城市
zhōngxīn dìqū , tèbié shì zhòngdiǎn yōngdǔ lùduàn , xiǎoqìchē
中心 地区，特别是 重点 拥堵路段，小汽车
yīnggāi yōuxiān ràng zìxíngchē tōngguò . Yěxǔ bù jiǔ , qí zìxíngchē
应该 优先 让 自行车 通过。也许不久，骑自行车
chūxíng , yòu huì biànchéng yì zhǒng xīn de shíshàng .
出行，又会 变 成 一 种 新的时 尚 。

策　　划：黄友义　王君校　韩　晖　付　眉
责任编辑：杨　晗
英文编辑：范逊敏　薛彧威
封面设计：何思倩

图书在版编目（CIP）数据

行在中国：汉英对照 / 李禄兴编著. -- 北京 ：华语教学出版社，2018.10
（当代中国微记录）
ISBN 978-7-5138-1639-7

Ⅰ. ①行… Ⅱ. ①李… Ⅲ. ①汉语－对外汉语教学－语言读物 Ⅳ. ①H195.5

中国版本图书馆CIP数据核字(2018)第226475号

行在中国

李禄兴　齐　影　编著
*
©华语教学出版社有限责任公司
华语教学出版社有限责任公司出版
（中国北京百万庄大街24号 邮政编码100037）
电话：(86)10-68320585 68997826
传真：(86)10-68997826 68326333
网址：www.sinolingua.com.cn
电子信箱：hyjx@sinolingua.com.cn
北京玺诚印务有限公司印刷
2019年（32开）第1版
2019年第1版第1次印刷
ISBN 978-7-5138-1639-7
定价：29.00元